THE BIG MEDITERRANEAN MEAL PREP UK COOKBOOK (FULL COLOUR PICTURES)

1200 Days Of Foolproof And Delicious Recipes With Weekly Diet Plans To Enjoy A

Beautiful And Healthy Lifestyle

LAVERNE S. SPICER

Table of Contents

Introduction 1

Chapter 1
Understanding the Mediterranean Diet 2
Principles of the Mediterranean Diet 3
Balanced eating approach is king in the Mediterranean Diet. 3
Eat beans, lentils, and whole grains regularly. 3
Cover half of our dinner plate with vegetables and fruits. 3
Use red meat as a flavoring or a complement to dishes rather than the main feature. 3
Foods To Focus On 3
Vegetables and fruits 3
Nuts and seeds 4
Olives and olive oil 4
Oily fish and seafood 4
Poultry, eggs, cheese, and yogurt 4
Foods To Cut Back On 5
Processed meats 5
Added sugars 5
Empty-calorie beverages 5
Refined grains 5

Chapter 2
Reasons for Choosing the Mediterranean Diet 6
Health Benefits of the Mediterranean Diet 7
Weight Maintenance Or Loss 7
Lower Risk of Metabolic Diseases 7
Lower Risk of Cancer 7
Lower Risk of Dementia and Alzheimer'S Disease 8
What Makes the Mediterranean Diet Different From Other Diets? 8
The Foods-- The Mediterranean diet has a food pyramid that allows any kind of food but places them in a hierarchical order. 8
The Lifestyle-- It's a holistic approach that teaches that to be truly healthy and happy, you need to feed your mind and your spirit as well as your body. 8

Chapter 3
Mediterranean Meal Planning 9
Meal-Planning Basics 10
Plan Meals You Love--If there's a recipe you're particularly fond of, use it as an entry point into meal planning. 10
Batch Cook And Freeze Meals---Batch cooking and freezing meals has saved many families from drive-thru food many times. 10
Use What You'Ve Got--- Go through your pantry, refrigerator, and freezer to figure out a meal. 10
The Balanced Plate 10
Start with ½ plate of vegetables. 11
Include a serving of healthy fat with each meal. 11
Satisfy your sweet tooth with fruit. 11

Chapter 4
4-Week Meal Plan 12
Week 1 13
Week 2 15
Week 3 17
Week 4 19

Chapter 5
Breakfast 21
Zesty Green Bites 22
Buttered Leeks with Poached Eggs 22
Cheesy Broccoli & Bell Pepper Frittata 22
C+C Overnight Oats 22
Funghi & Aglio Pizza 23
Pizza Quattro Formaggi 23
Courgette Muffins 23
Sunshine Overnight Oats 23
Scrambled Eggs with Goat Cheese and Roasted Peppers 24
Lemon Orzo with Fresh Herbs 24
Greek Yogurt Parfait 25
Greek Egg and Tomato Scramble 25
Breakfast Pita 26
Savory Sweet Potato Hash 26
Individual Baked Egg Casseroles 27
Overnight Pomegranate Muesli 27

Chapter 6
Snacks & Side Dishes 28
Baguette Bread 29
Basil Water Biscuits 29
Pistachio-Parmesan Kale-Rocket Salad 29

Easy Italian Orange and Celery Salad	29
Oven-Roasted Balsamic Beetroots	30
Spicy Roasted Potatoes	30
Mediterranean Crostini	30
Turkish-Spiced Nuts	30
Manchego Water Biscuits	31
Burrata Caprese Stack	31
Crispy Chili con carne Chickpeas	31
Crunchy Basil White Beans	31
Sea Salt Beetroot Chips	31
Herbed Labneh Vegetable Parfaits	32
Citrus Salad with Radicchio, Dates, and Smoked Almonds	32
Air Fryer Popcorn with Garlic Salt	32
Salmon-Stuffed Cucumbers	32

Chapter 7
Chicken and Poultry — 33

Chicken Meatballs in Tomato Sauce	34
Chicken with Steamed Artichokes	34
Valencian Chicken Paella	34
Hot Chicken with Black Beans	34
Chicken Risotto with Vegetables	35
Strawberry Turkey	35
Turkey Meatballs	35
Wild Rice and Kale Stuffed Chicken Thighs	35
Peach-Glazed Chicken Drummies	36
Baked Chicken Caprese	36
Lemon and Paprika Herb-Marinated Chicken	36
Chicken Kebabs with Tzatziki Sauce	37
Greek Chicken Burgers	37
Savory Chicken Meatballs	37
Greek Chicken Souvlaki	37
Whole Cornish Hen with Lemon and Herbs	38
Stovetop Chicken Cacciatore	38
Sautéed Chicken Cutlets with Romesco Sauce	38

Chapter 8
Beef, Lamb and Pork — 39

Pork Roast with Mushrooms Sauce	40
Pork Cutlets with Mushrooms in Tomato Sauce	40
Beans with Pancetta, Kale & Chickpeas	40
Crispy Beef with Rice	40
Short Ribs with Mushroom & Asparagus Sauce	41
Beef & Mushroom Steaks	41
Beef Sliders with Pepper Slaw	41
Mini Greek Meatloaves	42
Grilled Skirt Steak Over Traditional Mediterranean Hummus	42
Pressure Cooker Moroccan Pot Roast	42
Skirt steak with Artichokes	43
Spanish Pepper Steak	43
Pan-Fried Pork Cutlets with Peppers and Onions	43
Beef Stew with Green Peas	43
Moroccan Stuffed Peppers	44
Baked Lamb Kofta Meatballs	44
Roast Pork Tenderlon With Cherry-Balsamic Sauce	44
Pork Cutlets with Baby Carrots	44

Chapter 9
Fish and Seafood — 45

Potato Chowder with Hot Prawn	46
Italian Salmon with Creamy Polenta	46
Crabmeat with Asparagus & Broccoli Pilaf	46
Orange Salmon Fillets	46
Garlic-Lemon Salmon Steak	47
Lemon Pepper Prawn in Air Fryer	47
Lemon Garlic Prawn in Air Fryer	47
Parmesan Prawn	47
Juicy Air Fryer Salmon	48
Steamed Mussels in White Wine Sauce	48
Orange and Garlic Prawn	48
Paprika-Spiced Fish	48
Baked Jewfish with Cherry Tomatoes	49
Herbed Prawn Pita	49
Crushed Marcona Almond Swordfish	49
Greek Stuffed Squid	49

Chapter 10
Vegetarian Recipes — 50

Vegetarian Paella	51
Vegetable Stew	51
Stewed Kidney Bean	51
Lentil Spread with Parmesan	51
Broccoli & Orecchiette Pasta with Feta	52
Basil Tomatoes	52
Cheesy Spinach	52
Grilled Stuffed Portabello Mushrooms	52
Sautéed Garlic Spinach	53
Garlicky Sautéed Courgette with Mint	53
Freekeh, Chickpea, and Herb Salad	53
Kate's Warm Mediterranean Farro Bowl	53
Citrus French beans with Red Onions	53
Herbed Ricotta–Stuffed Mushrooms	54
Braised Greens with Olives and Walnuts	54
Crispy Lemon Artichoke Hearts	54
Spiced Honey-Walnut Carrots	54

Chapter 11
Desserts — 55

Vanilla & Walnut Cake	56
Vanilla Sweet Tortillas	56
Pumpkin & Walnut Sweet Rolls	56
Cinnamon & Lemon Apples	56
Lemon Fool	57
Roasted Orange Rice Pudding	57
Baklava and Honey	58
Date and Nut Balls	58
Chocolate Turtle Hummus	58
Avocado-Orange Fruit Salad	59
Shortbread with Strawberry Preserves	59
Orange–Olive Oil Fairy cakes	59
Olive Oil Ice Cream	59
Stuffed Figs with Goat Cheese and Honey	60
Lemon Panna Cotta With Blackberrles	60
Roasted Pears with Dried Apricots and Pistachios	60

Appendix 1 Measurement Conversion Chart	**61**
Appendix 2 The Dirty Dozen and Clean Fifteen	**62**
Appendix 3 Index	**63**

Introduction

The Mediterranean diet is a way of eating inspired by the traditional dietary patterns of countries surrounding the Mediterranean Sea. It emphasizes whole foods such as fruits, vegetables, whole grains, legumes, nuts and seeds, as well as healthy fats such as olive oil. The diet also includes moderate amounts of fish and poultry, and limited amounts of dairy products, red meat, and sweets. The focus is on using healthy, minimally processed ingredients to create flavorful and satisfying meals. This way of eating has been associated with numerous health benefits, including improved heart health, weight management, and decreased risk of chronic diseases.

Chapter 1: Understanding the Mediterranean Diet

Principles of the Mediterranean Diet

Balanced eating approach is king in the Mediterranean Diet.

The balanced eating approach is indeed the king of the Mediterranean diet. The focus is on consuming a variety of nutrient-dense foods in moderation, rather than limiting or eliminating any one food group. This approach promotes overall health and wellness and has been associated with numerous health benefits, including improved heart health, weight management, and decreased risk of chronic diseases. The Mediterranean diet is not a strict regimen, but rather a flexible way of eating that can be adapted to meet individual needs and preferences.

Eat beans, lentils, and whole grains regularly.

Beans, lentils, and whole grains are an important part of the Mediterranean diet. These foods provide fiber, protein, and complex carbohydrates, which can help to keep you full and satisfied. They also offer a range of vitamins and minerals, including iron, zinc, and B-vitamins. Eating beans, lentils, and whole grains regularly can help to promote overall health and wellness and has been associated with numerous health benefits, including improved heart health and decreased risk of chronic diseases. In the Mediterranean diet, these foods are typically consumed as part of a balanced eating approach that includes a variety of nutritious foods, rather than as the sole focus.

Cover half of our dinner plate with vegetables and fruits.

it is typical to include a generous serving of fruits and vegetables in the Mediterranean diet. In fact, filling half of your dinner plate with these foods is a great way to ensure that you are getting a good balance of nutrients and staying within the guidelines of the Mediterranean diet. Fruits and vegetables are high in fiber, vitamins, and minerals, and low in calories, making them an ideal choice for a healthy diet. They also provide antioxidants and phytochemicals that can help to protect against chronic diseases. The Mediterranean diet emphasizes a variety of colorful and flavorful produce, and encourages the use of seasonal and local ingredients.

Use red meat as a flavoring or a complement to dishes rather than the main feature.

Red meat is typically consumed in limited amounts in the Mediterranean diet. It is often used as a flavoring or a complement to dishes, rather than as the main feature. This is in line with the overall approach of the Mediterranean diet, which emphasizes a balanced eating pattern that includes a variety of nutritious foods, rather than focusing on any one food group. Red meat is a good source of protein, iron, and other nutrients, but it can also be high in saturated fat and cholesterol, so it is recommended to be consumed in moderation. The Mediterranean diet generally favors poultry, fish, and other seafood as the main sources of protein, and incorporates legumes, beans, and whole grains as alternative protein sources.

Foods To Focus On

Vegetables and fruits

There is a wide variety of fruits and vegetables that can be included in the Mediterranean diet. Some of the most commonly consumed include:

- Leafy greens such as spinach, kale, and Swiss chard
- Tomatoes and bell peppers
- Squash, eggplant, and zucchini
- Cucumbers, carrots, and radishes
- Artichokes, fennel, and asparagus
- Berries, including strawberries, blueberries, and blackberries
- Citrus fruits such as oranges, lemons, and grapefruit
- Apples, pears, and peaches
- Grapes and figs

The Mediterranean diet emphasizes using seasonal and local ingredients, so the specific fruits and vegetables you eat may vary depending on the time of year and your location. The focus is on consuming a variety of colorful and flavorful produce, and using ingredients that are minimally processed to create satisfying and nutritious meals.

Nuts and seeds

There is a wide variety of nuts and seeds that can be included in the Mediterranean diet, including:

- Almonds
- Walnuts
- Pistachios
- Hazelnuts
- Chia seeds
- Flaxseeds
- Sunflower seeds
- Pumpkin seeds
- Sesame seeds

Nuts and seeds are a great source of healthy fats, protein, fiber, and various vitamins and minerals. In the Mediterranean diet, they are often consumed as a snack, added to meals for extra crunch and flavor, or used as an ingredient in recipes such as salad dressings or baked goods. It is recommended to consume nuts and seeds in moderation, as they can be high in calories, but they can also help to reduce the risk of heart disease, diabetes, and other chronic conditions. The focus is on using a variety of nutritious ingredients in a balanced and flexible eating pattern.

Olives and olive oil

Olives and olive oil are staple ingredients in the Mediterranean diet. Olives are a good source of healthy fats, fiber, and vitamins, and can be enjoyed as a snack or added to a variety of dishes, such as salads or sandwiches. Olive oil is a key component of the Mediterranean diet and is used as a cooking oil, in dressings, and for dipping bread. Olive oil is rich in monounsaturated fats, which can help to lower cholesterol levels and reduce the risk of heart disease. In the Mediterranean diet, it is recommended to use extra-virgin olive oil, which is the least processed form of olive oil and has the highest concentration of beneficial nutrients.

The focus in the Mediterranean diet is on using healthy fats like olive oil in moderation, rather than limiting or eliminating any one food group. Olives and olive oil are used in a balanced and flexible approach to eating that emphasizes a variety of nutritious ingredients.

Oily fish and seafood

There is a wide variety of oily fish and seafood that can be included in the Mediterranean diet, including:

- Salmon
- Sardines
- Mackerel
- Tuna
- Anchovies
- Trout
- Shrimp
- Squid
- Scallops

Oily fish and seafood are excellent sources of omega-3 fatty acids, which have numerous health benefits, including reducing inflammation and improving heart health. They are also a good source of protein and other vitamins and minerals. In the Mediterranean diet, they are often consumed as a main course or as an ingredient in recipes, such as soups or stews. The focus is on consuming a variety of nutritious foods, including oily fish and seafood, in a balanced and flexible approach to eating.

Poultry, eggs, cheese, and yogurt

Poultry, eggs, cheese, and yogurt can all be included in the Mediterranean diet.

Poultry, such as chicken or turkey, is a good source of lean protein and can be prepared in a variety of ways, such as roasted, grilled, or stir-fried. Eggs are a versatile and nutritious food that can be cooked in a variety of ways, including boiled, fried, or baked.

Cheese and yogurt are both dairy products that can be included in the Mediterranean diet. Cheese, such as feta, goat cheese, or mozzarella, can be used as a topping for salads or as an ingredient in dishes like omelettes or pasta. Yogurt can be consumed on its own, used in smoothies or as a base for dips, or as an ingredient in baked goods.

In the Mediterranean diet, it is recommended to choose low-fat or non-fat dairy products, as they are lower in calories and saturated fat. The focus is on using a variety of nutritious ingredients in a balanced and flexible approach to eating.

Foods To Cut Back On

Processed meats

The Mediterranean diet emphasizes reducing the consumption of processed meats, such as sausage, ham, bacon, and deli meats. Processed meats are often high in sodium, preservatives, and other additives, and they have been linked to an increased risk of heart disease, cancer, and other health problems.

In the Mediterranean diet, it is recommended to limit the consumption of processed meats and instead focus on consuming a variety of whole, nutritious foods, including plenty of fruits, vegetables, whole grains, nuts and seeds, and healthy proteins like fish, poultry, and beans. The focus is on a balanced and flexible approach to eating that emphasizes the enjoyment of a wide variety of healthy, nutrient-dense foods.

Added sugars

In the Mediterranean diet, added sugars are limited or avoided as much as possible. Instead, natural sweeteners, such as honey or fruits, are used to add sweetness to recipes and snacks.

Added sugars are found in many processed foods and drinks, such as candy, baked goods, and sugary drinks. Consuming large amounts of added sugars can contribute to weight gain and increase the risk of chronic conditions, such as diabetes, heart disease, and tooth decay.

The Mediterranean diet emphasizes a whole foods approach, with an emphasis on minimally processed, natural ingredients. This helps to limit the amount of added sugars in the diet and provides a range of nutrients and health benefits. By focusing on a variety of nutrient-dense foods, the Mediterranean diet provides a balanced and flexible approach to eating that supports overall health and well-being.

Empty-calorie beverages

The Mediterranean diet emphasizes reducing the consumption of empty-calorie beverages, such as sugar-sweetened drinks and alcoholic beverages. These beverages are high in calories and sugar but low in nutrients, and they can contribute to weight gain, obesity, and other health problems.

Instead of empty-calorie beverages, the Mediterranean diet encourages the consumption of water, unsweetened tea, and coffee. These beverages are calorie-free and can help to hydrate the body. Wine is also a part of the Mediterranean diet, but it is consumed in moderation, with a focus on moderation, balance, and flexibility in overall food and beverage choices.

Refined grains

Refined grains, such as white bread, white rice, and pasta, are often stripped of their nutritious bran and germ during processing, leaving only the starchy endosperm. As a result, they have less fiber, vitamins, and minerals than whole grains.

In the Mediterranean diet, the focus is on incorporating more whole grains, such as whole wheat bread, brown rice, and quinoa, into your diet and cutting back on refined grains. Whole grains are a good source of fiber, vitamins, and minerals, and can help to improve heart health, control blood sugar levels, and promote digestive health.

The Mediterranean diet is a flexible and balanced approach to eating, so it's okay to include some refined grains in your diet, but it is recommended to prioritize whole grains most of the time. The focus is on incorporating a variety of nutritious ingredients in a way that works best for you and your health goals.

Chapter 2: Reasons for Choosing the Mediterranean Diet

Health Benefits of the Mediterranean Diet

Weight Maintenance Or Loss

The Mediterranean diet has been shown to be effective for both weight maintenance and weight loss. This is likely due to its focus on incorporating nutritious and filling foods, such as fruits and vegetables, whole grains, lean proteins, and healthy fats, into your diet.

Studies have found that people who follow the Mediterranean diet tend to have a lower body mass index (BMI) and a lower risk of obesity compared to those who do not follow this type of diet. Additionally, the Mediterranean diet has been shown to improve insulin sensitivity, which can help to regulate blood sugar levels and reduce the risk of type 2 diabetes.

Eating a variety of nutritious foods, rather than eliminating any one food group, is key to the Mediterranean diet. This approach to eating can help to prevent feelings of deprivation and increase long-term adherence to the diet, making it easier to maintain a healthy weight.

It's important to note that weight loss and weight maintenance are complex processes that depend on many factors, including genetics, lifestyle, and individual metabolism. However, incorporating the principles of the Mediterranean diet into your eating habits can be a helpful and healthy way to support your weight management goals.

Lower Risk of Metabolic Diseases

The Mediterranean diet has been shown to have many health benefits, including a lower risk of metabolic diseases such as type 2 diabetes, cardiovascular disease, and obesity.

Studies have shown that following a Mediterranean diet can help to improve insulin sensitivity, which is a key factor in the development of type 2 diabetes. It can also help to lower levels of "bad" LDL cholesterol and reduce inflammation, both of which are important factors in the development of cardiovascular disease.

In addition, the Mediterranean diet emphasizes eating a variety of healthy foods, including plenty of fruits and vegetables, whole grains, lean proteins, and healthy fats, which can help to promote a healthy weight and reduce the risk of obesity.

It's important to note that the Mediterranean diet is not a strict set of rules, but rather a flexible and balanced approach to eating that can be adapted to suit individual needs and preferences. By incorporating the principles of the Mediterranean diet into your eating habits, you can help to reduce your risk of metabolic diseases and improve your overall health and well-being.

Lower Risk of Cancer

Research suggests that following a Mediterranean diet may help to lower the risk of certain types of cancer. Some of the mechanisms by which the Mediterranean diet may help to reduce cancer risk include:

Antioxidant-rich foods: The Mediterranean diet is rich in antioxidants, which are substances that protect cells from damage caused by harmful molecules known as free radicals. This protection may help to reduce the risk of cancer.

Healthy fats: The Mediterranean diet emphasizes the use of healthy fats, such as olive oil, which have been shown to have anti-inflammatory properties that may help to reduce the risk of cancer.

Fiber: The Mediterranean diet is rich in fiber, which has been linked to a reduced risk of colon cancer.

Plant-based foods: The Mediterranean diet emphasizes plant-based foods, such as fruits, vegetables, nuts, and seeds, which are rich in vitamins, minerals, and phytochemicals that may help to protect against cancer.

It is important to note that while the Mediterranean diet may have health benefits, including a lower risk of cancer, it is not a guarantee. Other factors, such as genetics, lifestyle, and environment, can also play a role in cancer risk. Additionally, it is important to speak with your healthcare provider before making any changes to your diet, especially if you have a history of cancer or other health conditions.

Lower Risk of Dementia and Alzheimer'S Disease

Research has shown that following a Mediterranean diet is associated with a lower risk of dementia and Alzheimer's disease. The Mediterranean diet, which is rich in fruits, vegetables, whole grains, nuts, seeds, fish, and olive oil, and lower in red meat and dairy products, has been linked to improved cognitive function and a reduced risk of developing cognitive decline and dementia.

There are several potential mechanisms by which the Mediterranean diet may provide protection against dementia and Alzheimer's disease, including reducing oxidative stress and inflammation, improving cardiovascular health, and promoting healthy blood flow to the brain.

While following a Mediterranean diet is not a guarantee of preventing dementia or Alzheimer's disease, it is one of several lifestyle factors that can contribute to maintaining cognitive health as we age. It is important to talk to your doctor about the best ways to promote brain health and reduce the risk of dementia, including incorporating a balanced diet, staying physically active, and engaging in mentally stimulating activities.

What Makes the Mediterranean Diet Different From Other Diets?

The Foods-- The Mediterranean diet has a food pyramid that allows any kind of food but places them in a hierarchical order.

The Mediterranean diet is unique in that it follows a food pyramid, which provides guidelines on the frequency of consumption of different food groups. Unlike other diets, the Mediterranean diet doesn't restrict any particular food group, but instead emphasizes eating a variety of nutritious foods in moderation.

The food pyramid, also known as the Mediterranean Diet Pyramid, was created by Oldways, a non-profit organization, in collaboration with nutrition experts. It places the most emphasis on daily consumption of vegetables, fruits, whole grains, and legumes, followed by moderate amounts of fish, poultry, eggs, dairy, and sweets, and less frequent consumption of red meat and processed foods.

The Mediterranean diet food pyramid provides a flexible and balanced approach to eating, allowing for individual variation based on personal preferences and cultural food traditions. It encourages a lifestyle approach to eating and promotes the enjoyment of food as part of a healthy and fulfilling life. This is what makes the Mediterranean diet different from other diets, as it is less restrictive and more focused on promoting a healthy relationship with food.

The Lifestyle-- It's a holistic approach that teaches that to be truly healthy and happy, you need to feed your mind and your spirit as well as your body.

The Mediterranean diet is not just about what you eat, but also about the way you eat, the culture, and the lifestyle. The Mediterranean way of life prioritizes social connections, physical activity, and a sense of purpose.

In the Mediterranean diet, food is seen as more than just fuel, it's also a source of pleasure, enjoyment, and celebration. Eating is a communal experience, and meals are typically shared with family and friends. Physical activity is also an important part of the Mediterranean lifestyle, and can include activities such as walking, swimming, and gardening.

This holistic approach, which recognizes the importance of feeding the mind, spirit, and body, is what sets the Mediterranean diet apart from other diets that focus solely on reducing calorie intake or cutting out certain foods. By focusing on a balanced and flexible approach to eating and lifestyle, the Mediterranean diet can promote not just physical health, but also mental and emotional well-being.

Chapter 3
Mediterranean Meal Planning

Meal-Planning Basics

Plan Meals You Love--If there's a recipe you're particularly fond of, use it as an entry point into meal planning.

When you plan meals that you love, it makes it easier to stick to your meal plan and enjoy the foods you're eating. You can also try experimenting with new recipes that incorporate ingredients from the Mediterranean diet, such as olive oil, whole grains, vegetables, and seafood.

Incorporating a variety of flavors and ingredients can help keep your meals interesting and prevent boredom, and it's also a great way to get creative in the kitchen and try new things.

It's important to remember that the Mediterranean diet is a flexible and balanced approach to eating, so there's no need to restrict yourself to only eating foods that are traditionally part of the diet. The key is to find a way to incorporate more nutritious ingredients into your meals in a way that works for you and your taste preferences.

Batch Cook And Freeze Meals--Batch cooking and freezing meals has saved many families from drive-thru food many times.

Batch cooking and freezing meals can be a convenient and time-saving way to have healthy food on hand for busy days. It allows you to prepare several meals at once, store them in the freezer, and then simply reheat them when you're ready to eat.

Some good options for batch cooking and freezing include soups, stews, casseroles, pasta dishes, and grain bowls. These types of meals can often be easily portioned out and reheated, making them a quick and convenient option for busy weeknights or days when you don't have time to cook.

When batch cooking, it's important to store the food properly to ensure that it stays fresh and safe to eat. Use airtight containers and label them with the date and contents, and be sure to reheat the food thoroughly before eating.

Batch cooking and freezing meals can be a great way to save time and reduce food waste, while also making it easier to stick to a healthy eating plan like the Mediterranean diet.

Use What You've Got-- Go through your pantry, refrigerator, and freezer to figure out a meal.

Using what you already have on hand can help reduce waste, save money, and make the meal-planning process more efficient.

Before you start prepping, take inventory of your pantry, refrigerator, and freezer. Look for ingredients that need to be used up and consider incorporating them into your meal plan. You might be surprised by the delicious meals you can create simply by using what you have on hand.

You can also look for recipes that use similar ingredients to what you have available. For example, if you have a lot of vegetables in the fridge, you could make a stir-fry or a vegetable soup. If you have a surplus of grains, you could make grain bowls with different toppings.

Using what you've got is a great way to be mindful of food waste and make the most of the ingredients you have on hand. It can also make meal prepping more enjoyable and less stressful, as you'll have a starting point for your meals that takes the guesswork out of meal planning.

The Balanced Plate

The balanced plate is a concept that is central to the Mediterranean diet. It refers to a way of visualizing a healthy and balanced meal by dividing your plate into different sections, each representing a different food group.

A balanced plate on a Mediterranean diet might include:

Half of the plate filled with non-starchy vegetables, such as salads, roasted vegetables, or steamed greens.

A quarter of the plate filled with whole grains, such as brown rice, quinoa, or whole-grain bread.

A quarter of the plate filled with protein, such as fish, poultry, eggs, or legumes.

A small serving of healthy fats, such as olive oil, avocado, or nuts.

And, if desired, a small serving of fruit or dairy, such as yogurt or cheese.

By following the balanced plate concept, you can ensure that your meals are well-rounded and provide a good balance of nutrients to support overall health and well-being. The Mediterranean diet emphasizes the importance of variety and balance, so it's important to not only consider what you're eating, but also how you're eating it.

Start with ½ plate of vegetables.

starting with half a plate of vegetables is a great way to ensure that your meals are balanced and nutrient-dense when following the Mediterranean diet. Vegetables are rich in fiber, vitamins, and minerals, and can help you feel full and satisfied.

When meal prepping, you can start by prepping a variety of vegetables to have on hand for the week. Some good options for meal prepping include roasted or steamed vegetables, salads, and stir-fries.

You can also consider adding different seasonings, herbs, and spices to keep things interesting. For example, you could make roasted vegetables with olive oil, lemon, and garlic one day, and then add a different set of seasonings the next day, such as cumin and chili powder.

Starting with a base of vegetables in your meals is a great way to make sure that you're getting plenty of nutrients and fiber, and can help you feel full and satisfied, even with smaller portions of other food groups.

Include a serving of healthy fat with each meal.

Including a serving of healthy fats with each meal is an important part of the Mediterranean diet. Healthy fats help to provide long-lasting energy and support overall health, so they are an important part of any balanced meal plan.

Some examples of healthy fats to include in your meals are olive oil, avocados, nuts, and seeds. These fats can be added to meals in a variety of ways, such as drizzled over a salad, spread on whole grain bread.

When meal prepping, it's a good idea to have a variety of healthy fats on hand to add to your meals. For example, you could have a jar of olive oil, a bag of almonds, and a ripe avocado ready to go in your kitchen. That way, you can easily include a serving of healthy fats with each meal, even when you're on the go.

Remember, while healthy fats are an important part of a well-balanced diet, it's still important to be mindful of portion sizes. Consuming too much of any type of fat, even healthy fats, can lead to weight gain and other health problems.

Satisfy your sweet tooth with fruit.

Satisfying your sweet tooth with fruit is a healthy and delicious way to do so when following a Mediterranean diet.

Fruit is naturally sweet and provides important nutrients such as vitamins, minerals, and fiber. It can be enjoyed as a snack, dessert, or a sweet addition to a meal. Some popular fruit choices in the Mediterranean diet include:

Berries: strawberries, raspberries, blueberries, etc.

Stone fruits: peaches, plums, apricots, etc.

Citrus fruits: oranges, lemons, limes, etc.

Melons: watermelon, cantaloupe, honeydew, etc.

Incorporating fruit into your meal prep can be as simple as adding it to your breakfast, such as a bowl of yogurt with mixed berries, or making a fruit salad to have as a snack during the day. Dried fruit, such as apricots or figs, can also be a great addition to snacks or desserts.

Satisfying your sweet tooth with fruit is a great way to stay on track with your Mediterranean diet goals while also indulging your cravings for something sweet.

Chapter 4
4-Week Meal Plan

Week 1

Here is the following first week's meal plan for the Mediterranean diet. Try to follow the plan thoroughly to start getting the benefits of a Mediterranean diet.

Meal Plan	Breakfast	Lunch	Dinner	Snack
Day-1	Zesty Green Bites	Valencian Chicken Paella	Crispy Beef with Rice	Baguette Bread
Day-2	Funghi & Aglio Pizza	Spanish Pepper Steak	Orange Salmon Fillets	Baguette Bread
Day-3	Funghi & Aglio Pizza	Parmesan Prawn	Strawberry Turkey	Basil Water Biscuits
Day-4	Zesty Green Bites	Greek Stuffed Squid	Seafood Fideo	Basil Water Biscuits
Day-5	Pizza Quattro Formaggi	Juicy Air Fryer Salmon	Turkey Meatballs	Oven-Roasted Balsamic Beet-roots

Day-6	Courgette Muffins	Basil Tomatoes	Turkish-Spiced Nuts	Oven-Roasted Balsamic Beet-roots
Day-7	Zesty Green Bites	Spicy Roasted Potatoes	Burrata Caprese Stack	Oven-Roasted Balsamic Beet-roots

Week 2

Here is the following second week's meal plan for a Mediterranean diet. It's the second stage of the 4 weeks meal plan that you must take into account carefully.

Meal Plan	Breakfast	Lunch	Dinner	Snack
Day-1	Sunshine Overnight Oats	Greek Stuffed Squid	Spanish Pepper Steak	Baguette Bread
Day-2	Savory Sweet Potato Hash	Valencian Chicken Paella	Parmesan Prawn	Baguette Bread
Day-3	Zesty Green Bites	Orange Salmon Fillets	Crispy Beef with Rice	Oven-Roasted Balsamic Beetroots
Day-4	Buttered Leeks with Poached Eggs	Parmesan Prawn	Turkey Meatballs	Oven-Roasted Balsamic Beetroots
Day-5	Cheesy Broccoli & Bell Pepper Frittata	Basil Tomatoes	Crispy Beef with Rice	Olive Oil Ice Cream

Day-6	Pizza Quattro Formaggi	Turkey Meatballs	Turkish-Spiced Nuts	Olive Oil Ice Cream
Day-7	Courgette Muffins	Spicy Roasted Potatoes	Juicy Air Fryer Salmon	Olive Oil Ice Cream

Week 3

Here is the following third week's meal plan for a Mediterranean diet. In this stage, you already got the result of the previous two weeks' diet plan. So, follow this third stage of the meal plan completely to get a better result.

Meal Plan	Breakfast	Lunch	Dinner	Snack
Day-1	Cheesy Broccoli & Bell Pepper Frittata	Valencian Chicken Paella	Spiced Honey-Walnut Carrots	Basil Water Biscuits
Day-2	Cheesy Broccoli & Bell Pepper Frittata	Cheesy Spinach	Greek Stuffed Squid	Basil Water Biscuits
Day-3	Zesty Green Bites	Spicy Roasted Potatoes	Burrata Caprese Stack	Mediterranean Crostini
Day-4	Savory Sweet Potato Hash	Cheesy Spinach	Seafood Fideo	Mediterranean Crostini

Day-5	Pizza Quattro Formaggi	Valencian Chicken Paella	Spiced Honey-Walnut Carrots	Mediterranean Crostini
Day-6	Breakfast Pita	Orange Salmon Fillets	Spanish Pepper Steak	Pumpkin & Walnut Sweet Rolls
Day-7	Zesty Green Bites	Parmesan Prawn	Strawberry Turkey	Pumpkin & Walnut Sweet Rolls

Week 4

This is the final stage of our 4 week's Mediterranean diet meal plan. In this stage, you already have formed a habit of maintaining a Mediterranean diet. So, follow this final stage to get best the best result in your body and mind.

Meal Plan	Breakfast	Lunch	Dinner	Snack
Day-1	Courgette Muffins	Crunchy Basil White Beans	Turkey Meatballs	Mediterranean Crostini
Day-2	Zesty Green Bites	Mediterranean Crostini	Crunchy Basil White Beans	Mediterranean Crostini
Day-3	Buttered Leeks with Poached Eggs	Beef & Mushroom Steaks	Turkish-Spiced Nuts	Mediterranean Crostini
Day-4	Cheesy Broccoli & Bell Pepper Frittata	Burrata Caprese Stack	Beef & Mushroom Steaks	Manchego Water Biscuits
Day-5	Zesty Green Bites	Mediterranean Crostini	Juicy Air Fryer Salmon	Manchego Water Biscuits

Day-6	Breakfast Pita	Turkey Meatballs	Seafood Fideo	Manchego Water Biscuits
Day-7	Savory Sweet Potato Hash	Juicy Air Fryer Salmon	Beef & Mushroom Steaks	Manchego Water Biscuits

Chapter 5
Breakfast

Zesty Green Bites

Prep time: 5 minutes|Cook time:40 minutes|Serves 8

- ¼ cup frozen chopped kale
- ¼ cup finely chopped artichoke hearts
- ¼ cup ricotta cheese
- 2 tbsp grated Parmesan cheese
- ¼ cup goat cheese
- 1 large egg white
- 1 tsp dried basil
- 1 lemon, zested
- ½ tsp salt
- ½ tsp freshly ground black pepper
- 4 frozen filo dough, thawed
- 1 tbsp extra-virgin olive oil

1. In a bowl, combine kale, artichoke, ricotta, parmesan, goat cheese, egg white, basil, lemon zest, salt, and pepper.
2. Place a filo dough on a clean flat surface. Brush with olive oil.
3. Place a second filo sheet on the first and brush with more oil.
4. Continue layering to form a pile of four oiled sheets.
5. Working from the short side, cut the phyllo sheets into 8 strips and half them.
6. Spoon 1 tablespoon of filling onto one short end of every strip.
7. Fold a corner to cover the filling and a triangle; continue folding over and over to the end of the strip, creating a triangle-shaped filo packet.
8. Repeat the process with the other filo bites. Place a trivet into the pot.
9. Pour in 1 cup of water. Place the bites on top of the trivet.
10. Seal the lid and cook on High Pressure for 15 minutes. Do a quick release.

Buttered Leeks with Poached Eggs

Prep time: 5 minutes|Cook time:35 minutes|Serves 3

- 1 cup leeks, chopped into 1-inch pieces
- 6 eggs
- 2 tbsp oil
- 1 tbsp butter
- 1 tsp mustard seeds
- 1 tbsp dried rosemary
- ¼ tsp Chili con carne flakes
- ¼ tsp salt

1. Heat oil on Sauté and add mustard seeds.
2. Stir-fry for 2-3 minutes.
3. Add leeks and butter.
4. Cook for 5 minutes, stirring occasionally.
5. Crack eggs and season with dried rosemary, Chili con carne flakes, and salt. Cook until set, for about 4 minutes.
6. Press Cancel and serve immediately.

Cheesy Broccoli & Bell Pepper Frittata

Prep time: 5 minutes|Cook time:25 minutes|Serves 4

- 4 eggs
- 8 oz spinach, finely chopped
- ½ cup cheddar cheese
- ½ cup fresh ricotta cheese
- 3 cherry tomatoes, halved
- ¼ cup red bell pepper, chopped
- 1 cup chopped broccoli, pre-cooked
- 4 tbsp olive oil
- ½ tsp salt
- ¼ tsp freshly ground black pepper
- ¼ tsp dried oregano
- ½ cup fresh celery leaves, finely chopped

1. Heat olive oil on Sauté.
2. Add spinach and cook for 5 minutes, stirring occasionally.
3. Add tomatoes, peppers, and broccoli. Cook for more 3-4 minutes.
4. In a bowl, Whisk 2 eggs, cheddar, and ricotta.
5. Pour in the pot and cook for 2 more minutes.
6. Then, crack the remaining 2 eggs and cook for another 5 minutes.
7. When done, press Cancel.
8. Serve immediately with chopped celery leaves.

C+C Overnight Oats

Prep time: 5 minutes|Cook time:8 hours|Serves 2

- ½ cup vanilla, unsweetened almond milk (not Silk brand)
- ½ cup rolled oats
- 2 tablespoons rasherd almonds
- 2 tablespoons simple sugar liquid sweetener
- 1 teaspoon chia seeds
- ¼ teaspoon ground cardamom
- ¼ teaspoon ground cinnamon

1. In a mason jar, combine the almond milk, oats, almonds, liquid sweetener, chia seeds, cardamom, and cinnamon and shake well.
2. Store in the refrigerator for 8 to 24 hours, then serve cold or heated.

Funghi & Aglio Pizza

Prep time: 5 minutes|Cook time:20 minutes|Serves 2

- 1 cup flour
- ½ tsp brown sugar
- 1 tsp garlic powder
- 2 tsp dried yeast
- ¼ tsp salt
- 1 tbsp olive oil
- 1 cup water
- 1 cup button mushrooms, chopped
- ¼ cup Gouda, grated
- 2 tbsp tomato paste, sugar-free
- ½ tsp dried oregano
- ¼ cup lukewarm water

1. In a bowl fitted with a dough hook attachment, combine flour with brown sugar, dried yeast, and salt.
2. Mix well and gradually add lukewarm water and oil.
3. Continue to beat on high speed until smooth dough.
4. Transfer to a lightly floured surface and knead until completely smooth.
5. Form into a tight ball and wrap tightly in plastic foil. Set aside for one hour.
6. Line a baking dish with some greaseproof paper and set aside.
7. Roll out the dough with a rolling pin and transfer to the baking dish.
8. Brush with tomato paste and sprinkle with oregano, gouda, and button mushrooms.
9. Add a trivet inside your Instant Pot and pour in 1 cup of water.
10. Put the dish on the trivet. Seal the lid, and cook for 15 minutes on High Pressure. Do a quick release.
11. Remove the pizza from the pot using a greaseproof paper. Cut and serve.

Pizza Quattro Formaggi

Prep time: 5 minutes|Cook time:320 minutes|Serves 4

- 1 pizza crust
- ½ cup tomato paste
- ¼ cup water
- 1 tsp dried oregano
- 1 oz cheddar cheese
- 5-6 rashers mozzarella
- ¼ cup grated gouda
- ¼ cup grated parmesan
- ½ cup grated gouda cheese
- 2 tbsp extra virgin olive oil

1. Grease the bottom of a baking dish with one tablespoon of olive oil.
2. Line some greaseproof paper.
3. Flour the working surface and roll out the pizza dough to the approximate size of your instant pot.
4. Gently fit the dough in the previously prepared baking dish.
5. In a small bowl, combine tomato paste with water, and dry oregano.

6. Spread the mixture over dough and finish with cheeses.
7. Add a trivet inside your the pot and pour in 1 cup of water.
8. Seal the lid, and cook for 15 minutes on High Pressure.
9. Do a quick release.
10. Remove the pizza from the pot using a greaseproof paper.
11. Cut and serve.

Courgette Muffins

Prep time: 10 minutes|Cook time:20 minutes|Serves 8

- 1½ cups uncooked bulgur
- 2 cups 2% milk
- 1 cup water
- ½ teaspoon ground cinnamon
- 2 cups frozen (or fresh, pitted) dark sweet cherries
- 8 dried (or fresh) figs, chopped
- ½ cup chopped almonds
- ¼ cup loosely packed fresh mint, chopped
- Warm 2% milk, for serving (optional)

1. In a medium saucepan, combine the bulgur, milk, water, and cinnamon.
2. Stir once, then bring just to a boil.
3. Cover, reduce the heat to medium-low, and simmer for 10 minutes or until the liquid is absorbed.
4. Turn off the heat, but keep the pan on the stove, and stir in the frozen cherries (no need to thaw), figs, and almonds.
5. Stir well, cover for 1 minute, and let the hot bulgur thaw the cherries and partially hydrate the figs. Stir in the mint.
6. Scoop into serving bowls.
7. Serve with warm milk, if desired. You can also serve it chilled.

Sunshine Overnight Oats

Prep time: 5 minutes|Cook time:8 hours|Serves 2

- ⅔ cup vanilla, unsweetened almond milk (not Silk brand)
- ⅓ cup rolled oats
- ¼ cup raspberries
- 1 teaspoon honey
- ¼ teaspoon turmeric
- ⅛ teaspoon ground cinnamon
- Pinch ground cloves

1. In a mason jar, combine the almond milk, oats, raspberries, honey, turmeric, cinnamon, and cloves and shake well.
2. Store in the refrigerator for 8 to 24 hours, then serve cold or heated.

Scrambled Eggs with Goat Cheese and Roasted Peppers

Prep time: 5 minutes|Cook time:35 minutes|Serves 4

- 1½ teaspoons extra-virgin olive oil
- 1 cup chopped capsicums, any color (about 1 medium pepper)
- 2 garlic cloves, minced (about 1 teaspoon)
- 6 large eggs
- ¼ teaspoon kosher or sea salt
- 2 tablespoons water
- ½ cup crumbled goat cheese (about 2 ounces)
- 2 tablespoons loosely packed chopped fresh mint

1. In a large frying pan over medium-high heat, heat the oil.
2. Add the peppers and cook for 5 minutes, stirring occasionally.
3. Add the garlic and cook for 1 minute.
4. While the peppers are cooking, in a medium bowl, whisk together the eggs, salt, and water.
5. Turn the heat down to medium-low.
6. Pour the egg mixture over the peppers. Let the eggs cook undisturbed for 1 to 2 minutes, until they begin to set on the bottom.
7. Sprinkle with the goat cheese.
8. Cook the eggs for about 1 to 2 more minutes, stirring slowly, until the eggs are soft-set and custardy. (They will continue to cook off the stove from the residual heat in the pan.)
9. Top with the fresh mint and serve.

Lemon Orzo with Fresh Herbs

Prep time: 10 minutes|Cook time:10 minutes|Serves 4

- 2 cups orzo
- ½ cup fresh parsley, finely chopped
- ½ cup fresh basil, finely chopped
- 2 tablespoons lemon zest
- ½ cup extra-virgin olive oil
- ⅓ cup lemon juice
- 1 teaspoon salt
- ½ teaspoon freshly ground black pepper

1. Bring a large pot of water to a boil.
2. Add the orzo and cook for 7 minutes.
3. Drain and rinse with cold water. Let the orzo sit in a sieveer to completely drain and cool.
4. Once the orzo has cooled, put it in a large bowl and add the parsley, basil, and lemon zest.
5. In a small bowl, whisk together the olive oil, lemon juice, salt, and pepper.
6. Add the dressing to the pasta and toss everything together.
7. Serve at room temperature or chilled.

Greek Yogurt Parfait

Prep time: 5 minutes|Cook time:35 minutes|Serves 1

- ½ cup plain whole-milk Greek yogurt
- 2 tablespoons heavy whipping cream
- ¼ cup frozen berries, thawed with juices
- ½ teaspoon vanilla or almond extract (optional)
- ¼ teaspoon ground cinnamon (optional)
- 1 tablespoon ground flaxseed
- 2 tablespoons chopped nuts (walnuts or pecans)

1. In a small bowl or glass, combine the yogurt, heavy whipping cream, thawed berries in their juice, vanilla or almond extract (if using), cinnamon (if using), and flaxseed and stir well until smooth.
2. Top with chopped nuts and enjoy.

Greek Egg and Tomato Scramble

Prep time: 10 minutes|Cook time:25 minutes|Serves 4

- ¼ cup extra-virgin olive oil, divided
- 1½ cups chopped fresh tomatoes
- ¼ cup finely minced red onion
- 2 garlic cloves, minced
- ½ teaspoon dried oregano or 1 to 2 teaspoons chopped fresh oregano
- ½ teaspoon dried thyme or 1 to 2 teaspoons chopped fresh thyme
- 8 large eggs
- ½ teaspoon salt
- ¼ teaspoon freshly ground black pepper
- ¾ cup crumbled feta cheese
- ¼ cup chopped fresh mint leaves

1. In large frying pan, heat the olive oil over medium heat.
2. Add the chopped tomatoes and red onion and sauté until tomatoes are cooked through and soft, 10 to 12 minutes.
3. Add the garlic, oregano, and thyme and sauté another 2 to 4 minutes, until fragrant and liquid has reduced.
4. In a medium bowl, whisk together the eggs, salt, and pepper until well combined.
5. Add the eggs to the frying pan, reduce the heat to low, and scramble until set and creamy, using a spatula to move them constantly, 3 to 4 minutes.
6. Remove the frying pan from the heat, stir in the feta and mint, and serve warm.

Breakfast Pita

Prep time: 5 minutes|Cook time:6 minutes|Serves 2

- 1 whole wheat pita
- 2 teaspoons olive oil
- ½ shallot, diced
- ¼ teaspoon garlic, minced
- 1 large egg
- ¼ teaspoon dried oregano
- ¼ teaspoon dried thyme
- ⅛ teaspoon salt
- 2 tablespoons shredded Parmesan cheese

1. Preheat the air fryer to 190 .
2. Brush the top of the pita with olive oil, then spread the diced shallot and minced garlic over the pita.
3. Crack the egg into a small bowl or ramekin, and season it with oregano, thyme, and salt.
4. Place the pita into the air fryer basket, and gently pour the egg onto the top of the pita.
5. Sprinkle with cheese over the top.
6. Bake for 6 minutes.
7. Allow to cool for 5 minutes before cutting into pieces for serving.

Savory Sweet Potato Hash

Prep time: 15 minutes|Cook time:18 minutes|Serves 6

- 2 medium sweet potatoes, peeled and cut into 1-inch cubes
- ½ green bell pepper, diced
- ½ red onion, diced
- 4 ounces baby bella mushrooms, diced
- 2 tablespoons olive oil
- 1 garlic clove, minced
- ½ teaspoon salt
- ½ teaspoon black pepper
- ½ tablespoon chopped fresh rosemary

1. Preheat the air fryer to 190 .
2. In a large bowl, toss all ingredients together until the vegetables are well coated and seasonings distributed.
3. Pour the vegetables into the air fryer basket, making sure they are in a single even layer. (If using a smaller air fryer, you may need to do this in two batches.)
4. Cook for 9 minutes, then toss or flip the vegetables. Cook for 9 minutes more.
5. Transfer to a serving bowl or individual plates and enjoy.

Individual Baked Egg Casseroles

Prep time: 10 minutes|Cook time:30 minutes|Serves 2

- 1 rasher whole-grain bread
- 4 large eggs, beaten
- 3 tablespoons milk
- ¼ teaspoon salt
- ½ teaspoon onion powder
- ¼ teaspoon garlic powder
- Pinch freshly ground black pepper
- ¾ cup chopped vegetables (any kind you like—e.g., cherry tomatoes, mushrooms, spring onions, spinach, broccoli, etc.)

1. Heat the oven to 165 and set the rack to the middle position.
2. Oil two 8-ounce ramekins and place them on a baking tray.
3. Tear the bread into pieces and line each ramekin with ½ of a rasher.
4. Mix the eggs, milk, salt, onion powder, garlic powder, pepper, and vegetables in a medium bowl.
5. Pour half of the egg mixture into each ramekin.
6. Bake for 30 minutes, or until the eggs are set.

Overnight Pomegranate Muesli

Prep time: 10 minutes|Cook time:30 minutes|Serves 2

- ½ cup gluten-free old-fashioned oats
- ¼ cup shelled pistachios
- 3 tablespoons pumpkin seeds
- 2 tablespoons chia seeds
- ¾ cup milk
- ½ cup plain Greek yogurt
- 2 to 3 teaspoons maple syrup (optional)
- ½ cup pomegranate arils

1. In a medium bowl, mix together the oats, pistachios, pumpkin seeds, chia seeds, milk, yogurt, and maple syrup, if using.
2. Divide the mixture between two 12-ounce mason jars or another type of container with a lid.
3. Top each with ¼ cup of pomegranate arils.
4. Cover each jar or container and store in the refrigerator overnight or up to 4 days.
5. Serve cold, with additional milk if desired.

Chapter 6
Snacks & Side Dishes

Baguette Bread

Prep time: 15 minutes|Cook time:20 minutes|Serves 8

- ¾ cup warm water
- 1 cup strong flour
- ½ cup whole-wheat flour
- ½ cup oat flour
- ½ teaspoon sugar
- ¾ teaspoon quick yeast
- 1¼ teaspoons salt

1. In a large bowl, add the warm water and sprinkle with yeast and sugar.
2. Set aside for five minutes until foamy.
3. Add the strong flour and salt, and mix until a stiff dough forms.
4. Put the dough onto a floured surface and knead until smooth and elastic.
5. Then, shape the dough into a ball. Place the dough into a bowl with some oil and turn to coat well.
6. With cling film, cover the bowl and place it in a warm place for about 1 hour.
7. Punch down the dough and form it into a long slender loaf.
8. Place the loaf onto a lightly greased baking tray and set aside in a warm place, uncovered, for about 30 minutes.
9. Select the "Bake" mode. Set the cooking time to twenty minutes. Set the temperature at 220° F.
10. Arrange the dough onto the "Wire Rack" and insert it in the oven. Invert the bread onto the wire rack to cool before slicing.

Basil Water Biscuits

Prep time: 10 minutes|Cook time:17 minutes|Serves 6

- ½ tsp. baking powder
- Salt and black pepper to taste
- One and ¼ cups wholemeal flour
- ¼ tsp. basil, dried
- One garlic clove, minced
- 2 tbsp. basil pesto
- 2 tbsp. olive oil

1. In a bowl, mix flour with salt, pepper, baking powder, garlic, cayenne, basil, pesto, and oil.
2. Stir until you obtain a dough and spread it on a lined baking tray.
3. Introduce in the Air Fryer at 155° F and bake for 17 minutes.
4. Allow to cool, cut into Water biscuits and serve as a snack.

Pistachio-Parmesan Kale-Rocket Salad

Prep time: 20 minutes|Cook time:0 minutes|Serves 6

- 6 cups raw kale, center ribs removed and discarded, leaves coarsely chopped
- ¼ cup extra-virgin olive oil
- 2 tablespoons freshly squeezed lemon juice (from about 1 small lemon)
- ½ teaspoon smoked paprika
- 2 cups rocket
- ⅓ cup unsalted shelled pistachios
- 6 tablespoons grated Parmesan or Pecorino Romano cheese

1. In a large salad bowl, combine the kale, oil, lemon juice, and smoked paprika.
2. With your hands, gently massage the leaves for about 15 seconds or so, until all are thoroughly coated.
3. Let the kale sit for 10 minutes.
4. When you're ready to serve, gently mix in the rocket and pistachios.
5. Divide the salad among six serving bowls, sprinkle 1 tablespoon of grated cheese over each, and serve.

Easy Italian Orange and Celery Salad

Prep time: 15 minutes|Cook time:0 minutes|Serves 6

- 3 celery stalks, including leaves, rasherd diagonally into ½-inch rashers
- 2 large oranges, peeled and rasherd into rounds
- ½ cup green olives (or any variety)
- ¼ cup rasherd red onion (about ¼ onion)
- 1 tablespoon extra-virgin olive oil
- 1 tablespoon olive brine
- 1 tablespoon freshly squeezed lemon or orange juice (from ½ small lemon or 1 orange round)
- ¼ teaspoon kosher or sea salt
- ¼ teaspoon freshly ground black pepper

1. Place the celery, oranges, olives, and onion on a large serving platter or in a shallow, wide bowl.
2. In a small bowl, whisk together the oil, olive brine, and lemon juice.
3. Pour over the salad, sprinkle with salt and pepper, and serve.

Oven-Roasted Balsamic Beetroots

Prep time: 20 minutes|Cook time:40 minutes|Serves 8 to 10

- 10 medium fresh Beetroots
- 4 tablespoons extra-virgin olive oil, divided
- 1 teaspoon salt
- 3 teaspoons fresh thyme leaves, stems removed
- ⅓ cup balsamic vinegar
- ½ teaspoon freshly ground black pepper

1. Preheat the oven to 200 .
2. Cut off the stems and roots of the Beetroots. Wash the Beetroots thoroughly and dry them with a paper towel.
3. Peel the Beetroots using a vegetable peeler. Cut the Beetroots into ½-inch pieces and put them into a large bowl.
4. Add 2 tablespoons of olive oil, the salt, and thyme to the bowl. Toss together and pour out onto a baking tray. Spread the Beetroots so that they are evenly distributed.
5. Bake for 35 to 40 minutes, turning once or twice with a spatula, until the Beetroots are tender.
6. When the Beetroots are done cooking, set them aside and let cool for 10 minutes.
7. In a small bowl, whisk together the remaining olive oil, vinegar, and black pepper.
8. Transfer the Beetroots into a serving bowl, spoon the vinegar mixture over the Beetroots, and serve.

Spicy Roasted Potatoes

Prep time: 20 minutes|Cook time:25 minutes|Serves 5

- 1½ pounds red potatoes or gold potatoes
- 3 tablespoons garlic, minced
- 1½ teaspoons salt
- ¼ cup extra-virgin olive oil
- ½ cup fresh coriander, fresh, chopped
- ½ teaspoon freshly ground black pepper
- ¼ teaspoon cayenne pepper
- 3 tablespoons lemon juice

1. Preheat the oven to 220 .
2. Scrub the potatoes and pat dry.
3. Cut the potatoes into ½-inch pieces and put them into a bowl.
4. Add the garlic, salt, and olive oil and toss everything together to evenly coat.
5. Pour the potato mixture onto a baking tray, spread the potatoes out evenly, and put them into the oven, roasting for 25 minutes. Halfway through roasting, turn the potatoes with a spatula; continue roasting for the remainder of time until the potato edges start to brown.
6. Remove the potatoes from the oven and let them cool on the baking tray for 5 minutes.
7. Using a spatula, remove the potatoes from the pan and put them into a bowl.
8. Add the coriander, fresh, black pepper, cayenne, and lemon juice to the potatoes and toss until well mixed.
9. Serve warm.

Mediterranean Crostini

Prep time: 15 minutes|Cook time:10 minutes|Serves 6

- 1 baguette, rasherd ¼ inch thick
- 5 tablespoons extra-virgin olive oil
- ¼ teaspoon salt
- ⅛ teaspoon freshly ground black pepper
- ½ cup store-bought hummus or Garlic-Lemon Hummus
- 1 cup quartered grape tomatoes
- 1 cup diced cucumber
- 4 chopped pitted kalamata olives
- ½ cup crumbled feta cheese
- ½ cup chopped flat-leaf parsley, for garnish
- ⅓ cup Pickled Turnips (optional)

1. Preheat the oven to 170 .
2. On baking trays, arrange the baguette rashers and carefully brush the tops and sides with the oil.
3. Sprinkle with salt and pepper.
4. Bake for 10 minutes or until the toasts become slightly crispy.
5. Remove them from the oven and set aside.
6. Once the rashers are cool enough to handle, spread a thin layer of hummus on the toast.
7. Individually, spoon tomatoes, cucumber, olives, and feta cheese onto the toast. Garnish with fresh parsley and pickled turnips.

Turkish-Spiced Nuts

Prep time: 10 minutes|Cook time:5 minutes|Serves 4 to 6

- 1 tablespoon extra-virgin olive oil
- 1 cup mixed nuts (walnuts, almonds, cashews, ground nuts)
- 2 tablespoons paprika
- 1 tablespoon dried mint
- ½ tablespoon ground cinnamon
- ½ tablespoon flaked salt
- ¼ tablespoon garlic powder
- ¼ teaspoon freshly ground black pepper
- ⅛ tablespoon ground cumin

1. In a small to medium saucepan, heat the oil on low heat.
2. Once the oil is warm, add the nuts, paprika, mint, cinnamon, salt, garlic powder, pepper, and cumin and stir continually until the spices are well incorporated with the nuts.

Manchego Water Biscuits

Prep time: 15 minutes|Cook time:15 minutes|Serves 40

- 4 tablespoons butter, at room temperature
- 1 cup finely shredded Manchego cheese
- 1 cup almond flour
- 1 teaspoon salt, divided
- ¼ teaspoon freshly ground black pepper
- 1 large egg

1. Using an electric mixer, cream together the butter and shredded cheese until well combined and smooth.
2. In a small bowl, combine the almond flour with ½ teaspoon salt and pepper.
3. Slowly add the almond flour mixture to the cheese, mixing constantly until the dough just comes together to form a ball.
4. Transfer to a piece of parchment or cling film and roll into a cylinder log about 1½ inches thick. Wrap tightly and refrigerate for at least 1 hour.
5. Preheat the oven to 170 .
6. Line two baking trays with greaseproof paper or silicone baking mats.
7. To make the egg wash, in a small bowl, whisk together the egg and remaining ½ teaspoon salt.
8. Rasher the refrigerated dough into small rounds, about ¼ inch thick, and place on the lined baking trays.
9. Brush the tops of the Water biscuits with egg wash and bake until the Water biscuits are golden and crispy, 12 to 15 minutes.
10. Remove from the oven and allow to cool on a wire rack.
11. Serve warm or, once fully cooled, store in an airtight container in the refrigerator for up to 1 week.

Burrata Caprese Stack

Prep time: 5 minutes|Cook time:10 minutes|Serves 4

- 1 large organic tomato, preferably heirloom
- ½ teaspoon salt
- ¼ teaspoon freshly ground black pepper
- 1 (4-ounce) ball burrata cheese
- 8 fresh basil leaves, thinly rasherd
- 2 tablespoons extra-virgin olive oil
- 1 tablespoon red wine or balsamic vinegar

1. Rasher the tomato into 4 thick rashers, removing any tough center core and sprinkle with salt and pepper.
2. Place the tomatoes, seasoned-side up, on a plate.
3. On a separate rimmed plate, rasher the burrata into 4 thick rashers and place one rasher on top of each tomato rasher.
4. Top each with one-quarter of the basil and pour any reserved burrata cream from the rimmed plate over top.
5. Drizzle with olive oil and vinegar and serve with a fork and knife.

Crispy Chili con carne Chickpeas

Prep time: 5 minutes|Cook time:15 minutes|Serves 4

- 1 (15-ounce) can cooked chickpeas, drained and rinsed
- 1 tablespoon olive oil
- ¼ teaspoon salt
- ⅛ teaspoon Chili con carne powder
- ⅛ teaspoon garlic powder
- ⅛ teaspoon paprika

1. Preheat the air fryer to 190 .
2. In a medium bowl, toss all of the ingredients together until the chickpeas are well coated.
3. Pour the chickpeas into the air fryer and spread them out in a single layer.
4. Roast for 15 minutes, stirring once halfway through the cook time.

Crunchy Basil White Beans

Prep time: 2 minutes|Cook time:19 minutes|Serves 2

- 1 (15 ounce) can cooked white beans
- 2 tablespoons olive oil
- 1 teaspoon fresh sage, chopped
- ¼ teaspoon garlic powder
- ¼ teaspoon salt, divided
- 1 teaspoon chopped fresh basil

1. Preheat the air fryer to 190 .
2. In a medium bowl, mix together the beans, olive oil, sage, garlic, ⅛ teaspoon salt, and basil.
3. Pour the white beans into the air fryer and spread them out in a single layer.
4. Bake for 10 minutes.
5. Stir and continue cooking for an additional 5 to 9 minutes, or until they reach your preferred level of crispiness.
6. Toss with the remaining ⅛ teaspoon salt before serving.

Sea Salt Beetroot Chips

Prep time: 10 minutes|Cook time:30 minutes|Serves 6

- 4 medium Beetroots, rinse and rasherd thin
- 1 teaspoon sea salt
- 2 tablespoons olive oil
- Hummus, for serving

1. Preheat the air fryer to 190 .
2. In a large bowl, toss the Beetroots with sea salt and olive oil until well coated.
3. Put the Beetroot rashers into the air fryer and spread them out in a single layer.
4. Fry for 10 minutes. Stir, then fry for an additional 10 minutes. Stir again, then fry for a final 5 to 10 minutes, or until the chips reach the desired crispiness.
5. Serve with a favorite hummus.

Herbed Labneh Vegetable Parfaits

Prep time: 15 minutes|Cook time:10 minutes|Serves 2

- For the labneh
- 8 ounces plain Greek yogurt (full-fat works best)
- Generous pinch salt
- 1 teaspoon za'atar seasoning
- 1 teaspoon freshly squeezed lemon juice
- Pinch lemon zest
- For the parfaits
- ½ cup peeled, chopped cucumber
- ½ cup grated carrots
- ½ cup cherry tomatoes, halved

TO MAKE THE LABNEH

1. Line a sieveer with cheesecloth and place it over a bowl.
2. Stir together the Greek yogurt and salt and place in the cheesecloth. Wrap it up and let it sit for 24 hours in the refrigerator.
3. When ready, unwrap the labneh and place it into a clean bowl. Stir in the za'atar, lemon juice, and lemon zest.

TO MAKE THE PARFAITS

1. Divide the cucumber between two clear glasses.
2. Top each portion of cucumber with about 3 tablespoons of labneh.
3. Divide the carrots between the glasses.
4. Top with another 3 tablespoons of the labneh.
5. Top parfaits with the cherry tomatoes.

Citrus Salad with Radicchio, Dates, and Smoked Almonds

Prep time: 5 minutes|Cook time:10 minutes|Serves 4 to 6

- 2 red grapefruits
- 3 oranges
- 1 teaspoon sugar
- Salt and pepper
- 3 tablespoons extra-virgin olive oil
- 1 small shallot, minced
- 1 teaspoon Dijon mustard
- 1 small head radicchio (6 ounces), cored and rasherd thin
- ⅔ cup chopped pitted dates
- ½ cup smoked almonds, chopped coarse

1. Cut away peel and pith from grapefruits and oranges.
2. Cut each fruit in half from pole to pole, then rasher crosswise ¼ inch thick.
3. Transfer to bowl, toss with sugar and ½ teaspoon salt, and let sit for 15 minutes.
4. Drain fruit in fine-mesh sieveer set over bowl, reserving 2 tablespoons juice.
5. Arrange fruit on serving platter and drizzle with oil.
6. Whisk reserved juice, shallot, and mustard together in medium bowl.
7. Add radicchio, ⅓ cup dates, and ¼ cup almonds

and gently toss to coat.
8. Season with salt and pepper to taste.
9. Arrange radicchio mixture over fruit, leaving 1-inch border of fruit around edges.
10. Sprinkle with remaining ⅓ cup dates and remaining ¼ cup almonds. Serve.

Air Fryer Popcorn with Garlic Salt

Prep time: 2 minutes|Cook time:10 minutes|Serves 2

- 2 tablespoons olive oil
- ¼ cup popcorn kernels
- 1 teaspoon garlic salt

1. Preheat the air fryer to 190 .
2. Tear a square of Aluminium foil the size of the bottom of the air fryer and place into the air fryer.
3. Drizzle olive oil over the top of the foil, and then pour in the popcorn kernels.
4. Roast for 8 to 10 minutes, or until the popcorn stops popping.
5. Transfer the popcorn to a large bowl and sprinkle with garlic salt before serving.

Salmon-Stuffed Cucumbers

Prep time: 5 minutes|Cook time:10 minutes|Serves 4

- 2 large cucumbers, peeled
- 1 (4-ounce) can red salmon
- 1 medium very ripe avocado, peeled, pitted, and mashed
- 1 tablespoon extra-virgin olive oil
- Zest and juice of 1 lime
- 3 tablespoons chopped fresh coriander, fresh
- ½ teaspoon salt
- ¼ teaspoon freshly ground black pepper

1. Rasher the cucumber into 1-inch-thick segments and using a spoon, scrape seeds out of center of each segment and stand up on a plate.
2. In a medium bowl, combine the salmon, avocado, olive oil, lime zest and juice, coriander, fresh, salt, and pepper and mix until creamy.
3. Spoon the salmon mixture into the center of each cucumber segment and serve chilled.

Chicken Meatballs in Tomato Sauce

Prep time: 5 minutes|Cook time:30 minutes|Serves 5

- 1 pound ground chicken
- 3 tbsp red Chili sauce
- 1 egg
- ⅓ cup crumbled blue cheese
- ¼ cup bread crumbs
- ¼ cup Pecorino cheese
- 1 tbsp ranch dressing
- 1 tsp dried basil
- Salt and ground black pepper to taste
- 15 ounces Tinned tomato sauce
- 1 cup chicken broth
- 2 tbsp olive oil
- A handful of parsley, chopped

1. In a bowl, mix chicken, egg, pecorino, basil, pepper, salt, ranch dressing, blue cheese, 3 tbsp Chili sauce, and bread crumbs; shape the mixture into meatballs.
2. Warm oil on Sauté mode.
3. Add in the meatballs and cook for 2 to 3 minutes until browned on all sides.
4. Add in tomato sauce and broth. Seal the lid and cook on High Pressure for 7 minutes.
5. Release the pressure quickly. Remove meatballs carefully and place to a serving plate.
6. Top with parsley and serve.

Chicken with Steamed Artichokes

Prep time: 5 minutes|Cook time:30 minutes|Serves 5

- 1 lb chicken breasts, boneless, skinless, chopped
- 2 artichokes, trimmed, halved
- 2 tbsp butter, melted
- 2 tbsp olive oil
- 1 lemon, juiced
- Himalayan salt and black pepper to taste

1. Heat oil on Sauté and cook the chicken for a minute per side, until golden. Pour in 1 cup of water, seal the lid, and cook on High pressure for 13 minutes. Do a quick release. Set aside the chicken.
2. Place the trivet and pour a cup of water.
3. Rub the artichoke halves with half of the lemon juice, and arrange on top of the trivet.
4. Seal the lid and cook on Steam for 3 minutes on High. Do a quick release.
5. Combine artichoke and chicken in a large bowl.
6. Stir in salt, pepper, and lemon juice.
7. Drizzle butter over.

Valencian Chicken Paella

Prep time: 5 minutes|Cook time:25 minutes|Serves 4

- 4 boneless, skinless chicken legs
- 1 garlic clove, minced
- ½ tsp paprika
- ½ tsp turmeric
- 1 tsp cayenne pepper
- 1 tsp ground white pepper
- Salt to taste
- 1 tbsp oil olive
- 1 onion, chopped
- 1 tbsp tomato puree
- 2 cups chicken broth
- 1 cup long grain rice
- 1 celery stalk, diced
- 1 cup frozen green peas
- 1 red bell pepper, chopped
- Fresh parsley for garnish

1. Season chicken with garlic powder, white pepper, paprika, cayenne pepper, and salt.
2. Warm the oil on Sauté. Add in onion, garlic, and bell pepper; cook for 5 minutes.
3. Mix in tomato puree.
4. Add ¼ cup chicken stock into the cooker to deglaze the pan, scrape the pan's bottom to get rid of browned bits of food.
5. Mix in celery, rice, and the chicken.
6. Add in the remaining broth.
7. Seal the lid and cook on High Pressure for 8 minutes. Do a quick release.
8. Mix in green peas, cover with the lid and let sit for 5 minutes. Serve warm.

Hot Chicken with Black Beans

Prep time: 5 minutes|Cook time:25 minutes|Serves 4

- ½ cup chicken broth
- 3 tbsp honey
- 2 tbsp tomato paste
- ½ cup Chili sauce
- 3 garlic cloves, grated
- 4 boneless, skinless chicken drumsticks
- 1 tbsp cornflour
- 1 tbsp water
- 1 tbsp olive oil
- 2 cups Tinned black beans
- 2 spring onionss, thinly chopped

1. In the cooker, mix the Chili sauce, honey, tomato paste, chicken broth, and garlic.
2. Stir well until smooth; toss in the chicken to coat.
3. Seal the lid and cook for 3 minutes on High Pressure.
4. Release the Pressure immediately.
5. Open the lid and press Sauté. In a small bowl, mix water and cornflour until no lumps remain, Stir into the sauce and cook for 5 minutes until thickened.
6. Stir in olive oil and black beans; garnish with spring onionss and serve.

Chicken Risotto with Vegetables

Prep time: 5 minutes|Cook time:60 minutes|Serves 4

- 10 oz chicken breasts, boneless, skinless, cut into pieces
- 1 cup rice
- 6 oz button mushrooms, chopped, stems removed
- 1 red bell pepper, halved, seeds removed
- 1 green bell pepper, halved, seeds removed
- 1 yellow bell pepper, halved, seeds removed
- 6 oz broccoli, cut into florets
- ½ cup sweet corn
- 2 carrots, peeled and chopped
- 2 tbsp olive oil
- 1 tbsp butter
- 1 tsp salt
- ½ tsp freshly ground black pepper
- 1 tsp fresh basil, finely chopped
- Parmesan Cheese for topping

1. Add rice and pour in 3 cups of water.
2. Stir in butter, pepper and salt and seal the lid.
3. Cook on Rice mode for 8 minutes on High. Do a quick release and remove the rice.
4. Heat oil on Sauté, and add carrots and broccoli.
5. Sauté for 10 minutes. Add sweet corn and capsicums and cook for 5 minutes, stirring constantly.
6. Finally, stir in mushrooms, and cook for 3-4 minutes.
7. Remove the vegetables, mix with rice and set aside.
8. Add the chicken to the pot and pour in 2 cups of water.
9. Season with salt and pepper. Seal the lid and cook on High pressure for 7 minutes.
10. Do a quick release.
11. Open the lid, stir in rice and vegetables and serve warm sprinkled with Parmesan.

Strawberry Turkey

Prep time: 15 minutes|Cook time:25 minutes|Serves 2

- 2 lb. turkey breast
- 1 tbsp. olive oil
- 1 cup fresh strawberries
- Salt and pepper

1. Preheat your Air Fryer to 185 .
2. Massage the turkey breast with oil before seasoning with a generous salt and pepper pinch.
3. Cook the turkey in the Air Fryer for 15 minutes. Turn the turkey and cook for another 15 minutes.
4. Blend the strawberries in a food processor until smooth.
5. Pile the strawberries on top of the turkey and cook for another 7 minutes.

Turkey Meatballs

Prep time: 10 minutes|Cook time:20 minutes|Serves 6

- One lb ground turkey
- Two eggs, lightly beaten
- One tablespoon basil, chopped
- 1/3 cup coconut flour
- 1 tablespoon dried onion flakes
- Two cups Courgette, grated
- 1 teaspoon dried oregano
- 1 tablespoon garlic, minced
- 1 teaspoon cumin
- 1 tablespoon nutritional yeast
- Salt and Pepper

1. Select "Bake" to your Air Fryer and preheat to 190 for twenty minutes.
2. Add all ingredients into a bowl and mix until well combined.
3. Make small balls from the meat mixture, place them on a roasting pan and bake for twenty minutes.

Wild Rice and Kale Stuffed Chicken Thighs

Prep time: 10 minutes|Cook time:22 minutes|Serves 4

- 4 boneless, skinless chicken thighs
- 1 cup cooked wild rice
- ½ cup chopped kale
- 2 garlic cloves, minced
- 1 teaspoon salt
- Juice of 1 lemon
- ½ cup crumbled feta
- Olive oil cooking spray
- 1 tablespoon olive oil

1. Preheat the air fryer to 190 .
2. Place the chicken thighs between two pieces of cling film, and using a meat mallet or a rolling pin, pound them out to about ¼-inch thick.
3. In a medium bowl, combine the rice, kale, garlic, salt, and lemon juice and mix well.
4. Place a quarter of the rice mixture into the middle of each chicken thigh, then sprinkle 2 tablespoons of feta over the filling.
5. Spray the air fryer basket with olive oil cooking spray.
6. Fold the sides of the chicken thigh over the filling, and then gently place each of them seam-side down into the air fryer basket. Brush each stuffed chicken thigh with olive oil.
7. Roast the stuffed chicken thighs for 12 minutes, then turn them over and cook for an additional 10 minutes, or until the internal temperature reaches 75 .

Peach-Glazed Chicken Drummies

Prep time: 10 minutes|Cook time:20 minutes|Serves 6

- 8 chicken drumsticks (about 2 pounds), skin removed
- Nonstick cooking spray
- 1 (15-ounce) can rasherd peaches in 100% juice, drained
- ¼ cup honey
- ¼ cup cider vinegar
- 3 garlic cloves
- ½ teaspoon smoked paprika
- ¼ teaspoon kosher or sea salt
- ¼ teaspoon freshly ground black pepper

1. Remove the chicken from the refrigerator.
2. Set one oven rack about 4 inches below the broiler element.
3. Preheat the oven to 250 . Line a large, rimmed baking tray with Aluminium foil.
4. Place a wire cooling rack on the Aluminium foil, and spray the rack with nonstick cooking spray. Set aside.
5. In a blender, combine the peaches, honey, vinegar, garlic, smoked paprika, salt, and pepper.
6. Purée the ingredients until smooth.
7. Add the purée to a medium saucepan and bring to a boil over medium-high heat. Cook for 2 minutes, stirring constantly.
8. Divide the sauce among two small bowls. The first bowl will be brushed on the chicken; set aside the second bowl for serving at the table.
9. Brush all sides of the chicken with about half the sauce (keeping half the sauce for a second coating), and place the drumsticks on the prepared rack. Roast for 10 minutes.
10. Remove the chicken from the oven and turn to the high broiler setting.
11. Brush the chicken with the remaining sauce from the first bowl. Return the chicken to the oven and broil for 5 minutes.
12. Turn the chicken; broil for 3 to 5 more minutes, until the internal temperature measures 85 on a meat thermometer, or until the juices run clear.
13. Serve with the reserved sauce.

Baked Chicken Caprese

Prep time: 5 minutes|Cook time:25 minutes|Serves 4

- Nonstick cooking spray
- 1 pound boneless, skinless chicken breasts
- 2 tablespoons extra-virgin olive oil
- ¼ teaspoon freshly ground black pepper
- ¼ teaspoon kosher or sea salt
- 1 large tomato, rasherd thinly
- 1 cup shredded mozzarella or 4 ounces fresh mozzarella cheese, diced
- 1 (14.5-ounce) can low-sodium or no-salt-added crushed tomatoes
- 2 tablespoons fresh torn basil leaves
- 4 teaspoons balsamic vinegar

1. Set one oven rack about 4 inches below the broiler element.
2. Preheat the oven to 220 .
3. Line a large, rimmed baking tray with Aluminium foil.
4. Place a wire cooling rack on the Aluminium foil, and spray the rack with nonstick cooking spray. Set aside.
5. Cut the chicken into 4 pieces (if they aren't already).
6. Put the chicken breasts in a large zip-top plastic bag.
7. With a rolling pin or meat mallet, pound the chicken so it is evenly flattened, about ¼-inch thick.
8. Add the oil, pepper, and salt to the bag. Reseal the bag, and massage the ingredients into the chicken.
9. Take the chicken out of the bag and place it on the prepared wire rack.
10. Cook the chicken for 15 to 18 minutes, or until the internal temperature of the chicken is 85 on a meat thermometer and the juices run clear.
11. Turn the oven to the high broiler setting. Layer the tomato rashers on each chicken breast, and top with the mozzarella.
12. Broil the chicken for another 2 to 3 minutes, or until the cheese is melted (don't let the chicken burn on the edges).
13. Remove the chicken from the oven.
14. While the chicken is cooking, pour the crushed tomatoes into a small, microwave-safe bowl.
15. Cover the bowl with a paper towel, and microwave for about 1 minute on high, until hot.
16. When you're ready to serve, divide the tomatoes among four dinner plates.
17. Place each chicken breast on top of the tomatoes.
18. Top with the basil and a drizzle of balsamic vinegar.

Lemon and Paprika Herb-Marinated Chicken

Prep time: 10 minutes|Cook time:30 minutes|Serves 2

- 2 tablespoons olive oil
- 4 tablespoons freshly squeezed lemon juice
- ¼ teaspoon salt
- 1 teaspoon paprika
- 1 teaspoon dried basil
- ½ teaspoon dried thyme
- ¼ teaspoon garlic powder
- 2 (4-ounce) boneless, skinless chicken breasts

1. In a bowl with a lid, combine the olive oil, lemon juice, salt, paprika, basil, thyme, and garlic powder.
2. Add the chicken and marinate for at least 30 minutes, or up to 4 hours.
3. When ready to cook, heat the grill to medium-high (about 175–200) and oil the grill grate.
4. Alternately, you can also cook these in a nonstick sauté pan over medium-high heat.
5. Grill the chicken for 6 to 7 minutes, or until it lifts away from the grill easily.
6. Flip it over and grill for another 6 to 7 minutes, or until it reaches an internal temperature of 85 .

Chicken Kebabs with Tzatziki Sauce

Prep time: 45 minutes|Cook time:20 minutes|Serves 4

- ½ cup extra-virgin olive oil, divided
- ½ large lemon, juiced
- 2 garlic cloves, minced
- ½ teaspoon za'atar seasoning
- Salt
- Freshly ground black pepper
- 1 pound boneless skinless chicken breasts, cut into 1¼-inch cubes
- 1 large red bell pepper, cut into 1¼-inch pieces
- 2 small Courgette (nearly 1 pound), cut into rounds slightly under ½ inch thick
- 2 large shallots, diced into quarters
- Tzatziki Sauce

1. In a bowl, whisk together ⅓ cup of olive oil, lemon juice, garlic, za'atar, salt, and pepper.
2. Put the chicken in a medium bowl and pour the olive oil mixture over the chicken.
3. Press the chicken into the marinade.
4. Cover and refrigerate for 45 minutes.
5. While the chicken marinates, soak the wooden skewers in water for 30 minutes.
6. Drizzle and toss the pepper, Courgette, and shallots with the remaining 2½ tablespoons of olive oil and season lightly with salt.
7. Preheat the oven to 250 and put a baking tray in the oven to heat.
8. On each skewer, thread a red bell pepper, Courgette, shallot and 2 chicken pieces and repeat twice.
9. Put the kebabs onto the hot baking tray and cook for 7 to 9 minutes, or until the chicken is cooked through.
10. Rotate once halfway through cooking.
11. Serve the kebabs warm with the Tzatziki Sauce.

Greek Chicken Burgers

Prep time: 10 minutes|Cook time:10 minutes|Serves 2

- 1 pound ground chicken
- ¼ cup finely chopped red onion
- 3 tablespoons finely chopped red pepper
- 3 tablespoons crumbled feta cheese
- 3 tablespoons panko bread crumbs
- 1 garlic clove, minced
- ¼ teaspoon salt
- ⅛ teaspoon freshly ground black pepper
- Pita bread, for serving
- Pickled Onions, for serving
- Hummus, for serving

1. In a large bowl, combine the chicken, onion, peppers, feta, panko, garlic, oregano, salt, and pepper. Mix well and shape into 8 patties.
2. Preheat a grill to medium-high.
3. Grill the burgers for 4 to 5 minutes on each side, until the juices run clear and the patty is cooked through.
4. Serve on pita topped with pickled onions and hummus.

Savory Chicken Meatballs

Prep time: 20 minutes|Cook time:20 minutes|Serves 4

- 2 (1-pound) boxes frozen chopped spinach, thawed
- 1 medium shallot, grated
- 1 pound ground chicken
- ¾ cup crumbled feta cheese
- 2 tablespoons za'atar seasoning
- ¼ cup extra-virgin olive oil
- 4 whole-wheat pita bread rounds, for serving
- Tzatziki Sauce, for serving

1. Preheat the oven to 200 .
2. While the oven preheats, squeeze all the water out of the spinach until it's completely dry.
3. Use paper towels to blot it if necessary.
4. In a bowl, fluff the spinach with a fork to separate clumps and add the grated shallot to the spinach.
5. Combine all the ingredients and form the mixture into 10 to 15 meatballs. Lightly flatten the meatballs (just so that they won't roll around) and place on a nonstick baking tray.
6. Bake for 10 to 12 minutes, or until the meatballs are golden brown and cooked thoroughly.
7. Serve in a pita, topped with Tzatziki Sauce and cucumbers.

Greek Chicken Souvlaki

Prep time: 10 minutes, plus 1 hour|Cook time:15 minutes|Serves 4

- ½ cup extra-virgin olive oil, plus extra for serving
- ¼ cup dry white wine (optional; add extra lemon juice instead, if desired)
- 6 garlic cloves, finely minced
- Zest and juice of 1 lemon
- 1 tablespoon dried oregano
- 1 teaspoon dried rosemary
- ½ teaspoons salt
- ½ teaspoon freshly ground black pepper
- 1 pound boneless, skinless chicken thighs, cut into 1½-inch chunks
- 1 cup Tzatziki, for serving

1. In a large glass bowl or resealable plastic bag, combine the olive oil, white wine (if using), garlic, lemon zest and juice, oregano, rosemary, salt, and pepper and whisk or shake to combine well.
2. Add the chicken to the marinade and toss to coat.
3. Cover or seal and marinate in the refrigerator for at least 1 hour, or up to 24 hours.
4. In a bowl, submerge wooden skewers in water and soak for at least 30 minutes before using.
5. To cook, heat the grill to medium-high heat. Thread the marinated chicken on the soaked skewers, reserving the marinade.
6. Grill until cooked through, flipping occasionally so that the chicken cooks evenly, 5 to 8 minutes. Remove and keep warm.

Whole Cornish Hen with Lemon and Herbs

Prep time: 5 minutes|Cook time:45 minutes|Serves 4

- 1 (1½- to 2-pound) Cornish hen
- ¼ cup olive oil
- 2 tablespoons lemon juice
- 2 tablespoons fresh rosemary, chopped
- 2 tablespoons fresh thyme, chopped
- 4 garlic cloves, roughly chopped
- 1 teaspoon salt
- 1 teaspoon fresh ground black pepper
- 1 celery stalk, roughly chopped
- ½ small onion
- ½ lemon
- Chopped fresh parsley, for garnish
- Fresh cracked black pepper, for garnish

1. Preheat the air fryer to 190 .
2. In a small bowl, combine the olive oil, lemon juice, rosemary, thyme, garlic, salt, and pepper.
3. Brush the mixture over the tops and sides of the hen. Pour any excess inside the cavity of the bird.
4. Stuff the celery, onion, and ½ lemon into the cavity of the hen.
5. Place inside the air fryer basket and roast for 40 to 45 minutes, or until the internal temperature reaches 85 .
6. Cut the hen in half and serve with a sprinkle of parsley and fresh cracked black pepper.

Stovetop Chicken Cacciatore

Prep time: 15 minutes|Cook time:2 hours|Serves 2

- 1½ pounds bone-in chicken thighs, skin removed
- ½ teaspoon salt, divided
- 2 tablespoons olive oil
- ½ large onion, thinly rasherd
- 4 ounces baby bella mushrooms, rasherd
- 1 red sweet pepper, cut into 1-inch pieces
- 1 fresh rosemary sprig
- 1 (15-ounce) can crushed fire-roasted tomatoes
- ½ cup dry red wine
- 1 teaspoon Italian herb seasoning
- ½ teaspoon garlic powder
- 3 tablespoons flour

1. Pat the chicken dry and season it with a generous pinch of salt.
2. Heat the olive oil in a Dutch oven over medium-high heat. Add the chicken and cook for 5 minutes on each side, or until it's lightly browned all over.
3. Add the onion, mushrooms, and sweet pepper to the pot and sauté for 5 minutes more.
4. Add the rosemary, tomatoes, wine, Italian seasoning, garlic powder and remaining salt. Stir to combine.
5. Bring the mixture to a boil, then reduce the heat to low.
6. Let simmer slowly for at least 1 hour, and up to 2 hours, stirring occasionally, until the chicken is tender and easily pulls away from the bone.

7. Measure out 1 cup of the sauce from the pot and place it into a bowl.
8. Add the flour and whisk well to make a slurry.
9. Make sure it doesn't have any lumps.
10. Increase the heat to medium-high and slowly whisk the slurry back into the pot.
11. Stir until it comes to a boil and cook until the sauce thickens.
12. If desired, remove the chicken from the bones, shred it, and add it back to the sauce prior to serving.

Sautéed Chicken Cutlets with Romesco Sauce

Prep time: 5 minutes|Cook time:10 minutes|Serves 4

- Sauce
- ½ rasher hearty white sandwich bread, cut into ½ inch pieces
- ¼ cup hazelnuts, toasted and skinned
- 2 tablespoons extra-virgin olive oil
- 2 garlic cloves, rasherd thin
- 1 cup jarred roasted red peppers, rinsed and patted dry
- 1½ tablespoons sherry vinegar
- 1 teaspoon honey
- ½ teaspoon smoked paprika
- ½ teaspoon salt
- Pinch cayenne pepper
- Chicken
- 4 (4- to 6-ounce) boneless, skinless chicken breasts, trimmed
- Salt and pepper
- 4 teaspoons extra-virgin olive oil

1. FOR THE SAUCE Cook bread, hazelnuts, and 1 tablespoon oil in 12-inch frying pan over medium heat, stirring constantly, until bread and hazelnuts are lightly toasted, about 3 minutes.
2. Add garlic and cook, stirring constantly, until fragrant, about 30 seconds. Transfer mixture to food processor and pulse until coarsely chopped, about 5 pulses.
3. Add red peppers, vinegar, honey, paprika, salt, cayenne, and remaining 1 tablespoon oil to processor.
4. Pulse until finely chopped, 5 to 8 pulses.
5. Transfer sauce to bowl and set aside for serving. (Sauce can be refrigerated for up to 2 days.)
6. FOR THE CHICKEN Cut chicken horizontally into 2 thin cutlets, then cover with cling film and pound to uniform ¼-inch thickness.
7. Pat cutlets dry with paper towels and season with salt and pepper. Heat 2 teaspoons oil in 12-inch frying pan over medium-high heat until just smoking.
8. Place 4 cutlets in frying pan and cook, without moving, until browned on first side, about 2 minutes.
9. Flip cutlets and continue to cook until opaque on second side, about 30 seconds.
10. Transfer chicken to serving platter and tent loosely with Aluminium foil.
11. Repeat with remaining 4 cutlets and remaining 2 teaspoons oil.
12. Serve with sauce.

Pork Roast with Mushrooms Sauce

Prep time: 5 minutes|Cook time:60 minutes|Serves 6

- 2 lb pork shoulder
- 1 cup button mushrooms, chopped
- 2 tbsp butter, unsalted
- 1 tbsp balsamic vinegar
- ½ tsp garlic powder
- 1 tsp salt
- ¼ cup soy sauce
- 2 bay leaves
- 1 cup beef broth
- 2 tbsp cornflour

1. Rinse the meat and rub with salt and garlic powder.
2. Melt butter on Sauté. Brown the meat for 5 minutes on each side.
3. Stir in soy sauce and bay leaves.
4. Cook for 2 minutes before, add in beef broth and balsamic vinegar.
5. Seal the lid and set on Meat/Stew mode.
6. Cook for 30 minutes on High Pressure.
7. When done, do a quick release and stir in mushrooms.
8. Cook until tender, about 5 minutes, on Sauté mode.
9. Stir in cornflour and cook for 2 minutes.

Pork Cutlets with Mushrooms in Tomato Sauce

Prep time: 5 minutes|Cook time:30 minutes|Serves 4

- 4 large bone-in pork cutlets
- 1 cup tomato sauce
- 1½ cups white button mushrooms, rasherd
- 1 onion, chopped
- 1 tsp garlic, minced
- ½ cup water
- 1 tbsp oil
- Salt and black pepper, to taste

1. Heat oil on SAUTÉ.
2. Add garlic, onion and cook for 2 minutes, until soft and fragrant.
3. Add pork and cook until browned on all sides.
4. Stir in the remaining ingredients and seal the lid.
5. Cook for 20 minutes on MEAT/STEW mode at High.
6. When ready, do a quick pressure release.

Beans with Pancetta, Kale & Chickpeas

Prep time: 5 minutes|Cook time:25 minutes|Serves 8

- 5 cups Water, divided
- 1 pack (2 oz) Onion soup mix
- ¼ cup Olive Oil
- 1 tbsp Garlic, minced
- 1½ pounds Tinned Chickpeas, soaked overnight
- 2 tsp Mustard
- ½ pound Pancetta rashers, chopped
- 1 Onion, chopped
- 1 cup Kale, chopped

1. Heat the oil and cook the onions, garlic, and pancetta for 5 minutes on SAUTÉ mode.
2. Add 1 cup of water and the soup mix, and cook for 5 more minutes.
3. Then, add the chickpeas and 4 cups of water.
4. Add in the kale and mustard.
5. Seal the lid and cook for 15 minutes on Pressure Cook at High Pressure.
6. Once cooking is completed, perform a quick pressure release and serve immediately.

Crispy Beef with Rice

Prep time: 5 minutes|Cook time:50 minutes|Serves 4

- 2 lb beef shoulder
- 1 cup rice
- 2 cups beef broth
- 3 tbsp butter
- 1 tsp salt
- ½ tsp pepper

1. Rinse the meat and rub with salt.
2. Place it in the pot and pour in broth. Seal the lid and cook on Meat/Stew for 25 minutes on High Pressure.
3. Do a quick release, remove the meat but keep the broth.
4. Add rice and stir in 1 tbsp of butter. Seal the lid, and cook on Rice mode for 8 minutes on High.
5. Do a quick release.
6. Remove the rice and wipe the pot clean. Melt 2 tbsp of butter on Sauté.
7. Add meat and lightly brown for 10 minutes.
8. Serve with rice and season with pepper and salt.

Short Ribs with Mushroom & Asparagus Sauce
Prep time: 15 minutes|Cook time:1 hours|Serves 4

- 3½ pounds boneless beef short ribs, cut into pieces
- 2 tsp salt
- 1 tsp ground black pepper
- 3 tbsp olive oil
- 1 onion, diced
- 1 cup dry red wine
- 1 tbsp tomato puree
- 2 carrots, peeled and chopped
- 2 garlic cloves, minced
- 5 sprigs parsley, chopped
- 2 sprigs rosemary, chopped
- 3 sprigs oregano, chopped
- 4 cups beef stock
- 10 ounces mushrooms, quartered
- 1 cup asparagus, trimmed chopped
- 1 tbsp cornflour
- ¼ cup cold water

1. Season the ribs with black pepper and salt.
2. Warm oil on Sauté. In batches, add the short ribs to the oil and cook for 3 to 5 minutes each side until browned. Set aside.
3. Add onions and sauté for 4 minutes until soft.
4. Add tomato puree and red wine into the pot to deglaze, scrape the bottom to get rid of any browned beef bits.
5. Cook for 2 minutes until wine reduces slightly.
6. Return the ribs to the pot and top with carrots, oregano, rosemary, and garlic. Add in broth and press Cancel.
7. Seal the lid, press Meat/Stew and cook on High for 35 minutes.
8. Release Pressure naturally for 10 minutes. Transfer ribs to a plate.
9. Sieve and get rid of herbs and vegetables, and return cooking broth to inner pot.
10. Add mushrooms and asparagus to the broth.
11. Press Sauté and cook for 2 to 4 minutes until soft.
12. In a bowl, mix water and cornflour until cornflour dissolves completely.
13. Add the cornflour mixture into broth as you stir for 1 to 3 minutes until the broth thickens slightly.
14. Season the sauce with black pepper and salt.
15. Pour the sauce over ribs, add chopped parsley for garnish before serving.

Beef & Mushroom Steaks
Prep time: 5 minutes|Cook time:30 minutes|Serves 4

- 1 lb beef steaks
- 1 lb button mushrooms, thinly chopped
- 2 tbsp vegetable oil
- 1 tsp salt
- ½ tsp freshly ground black pepper
- 1 bay leaf
- 1 tbsp dried thyme

- 6 oz cherry tomatoes

1. Rub steaks with salt, pepper, and thyme.
2. Place in the instant pot.
3. Pour in 3 cups of water, add bay leaf and seal the lid.
4. Cook on High pressure for 13 minutes.
5. Do a quick release and set the steaks aside.
6. Heat oil on Sauté, and stir-fry mushrooms and tomatoes for 5 minutes.
7. Add steaks and brown on both sides.

Beef Sliders with Pepper Slaw
Prep time: 10 minutes|Cook time:10 minutes|Serves 4

- Nonstick cooking spray
- 1 (8-ounce) package white button mushrooms
- 2 tablespoons extra-virgin olive oil, divided
- 1 pound minced beef (93% lean)
- 2 garlic cloves, minced (about 1 teaspoon)
- ½ teaspoon kosher or sea salt, divided
- ¼ teaspoon freshly ground black pepper
- 1 tablespoon balsamic vinegar
- 2 capsicums of different colors, rasherd into strips
- 2 tablespoons torn fresh basil or flat-leaf (Italian) parsley
- Mini or slider whole-grain rolls, for serving (optional)

1. Set one oven rack about 4 inches below the broiler element.
2. Preheat the oven broiler to high.
3. Line a large, rimmed baking tray with Aluminium foil.
4. Place a wire cooling rack on the Aluminium foil, and spray the rack with nonstick cooking spray. Set aside.
5. Put half the mushrooms in the bowl of a food processor and pulse about 15 times, until the mushrooms are finely chopped but not puréed, similar to the texture of ground meat.
6. Repeat with the remaining mushrooms.
7. In a large frying pan over medium-high heat, heat 1 tablespoon of oil.
8. Add the mushrooms and cook for 2 to 3 minutes, stirring occasionally, until the mushrooms have cooked down and some of their liquid has evaporated.
9. Remove from the heat.
10. In a large bowl, combine the minced beef with the cooked mushrooms, garlic, ¼ teaspoon of salt, and pepper.
11. Mix gently using your hands.
12. Broil for 4 minutes. Flip the burgers and rearrange them so any burgers not getting brown are nearer to the heat source.
13. Broil for 3 to 4 more minutes, or until the internal temperature of the meat is 80 on a meat thermometer.
14. Watch carefully to prevent burning.
15. While the burgers are cooking, in a large bowl, whisk together the remaining 1 tablespoon of oil, vinegar, and remaining ¼ teaspoon of salt.
16. Add the peppers and basil, and stir gently to coat with the dressing.
17. Serve the sliders with the pepper slaw as a topping or on the side.
18. If desired, serve with the rolls, burger style.

Mini Greek Meatloaves
Prep time: 5 minutes|Cook time:25 minutes|Serves 6

- Nonstick cooking spray
- 1 tablespoon extra-virgin olive oil
- ½ cup minced onion (about ¼ onion)
- 1 garlic clove, minced (about ½ teaspoon)
- 1 pound minced beef (93% lean)
- ½ cup whole-wheat bread crumbs
- ½ cup crumbled feta cheese (about 2 ounces)
- 1 large egg
- ½ teaspoon dried oregano, crushed between your fingers
- ¼ teaspoon freshly ground black pepper
- ½ cup 2% plain Greek yogurt
- ⅓ cup chopped and pitted Kalamata olives
- 2 tablespoons olive brine
- Cos lettuce or pita bread, for serving (optional)

1. Preheat the oven to 200 . Coat a 12-cup muffin pan with nonstick cooking spray and set aside.
2. In a small frying pan over medium heat, heat the oil.
3. Add the onion and cook for 4 minutes, stirring frequently.
4. Add the garlic and cook for 1 more minute, stirring frequently. Remove from the heat.
5. In a large mixing bowl, combine the onion and garlic with the minced beef, bread crumbs, feta, egg, oregano, and pepper. Gently mix together with your hands.
6. Divide into 12 portions and place in the muffin cups.
7. Cook for 18 to 20 minutes, or until the internal temperature of the meat is 80 on a meat thermometer.
8. While the meatloaves are baking, in a small bowl, whisk together the yogurt, olives, and olive brine.
9. When you're ready to serve, place the meatloaves on a serving platter and spoon the olive-yogurt sauce on top.
10. You can also serve them on a bed of lettuce or with cut-up pieces of pita bread.

Grilled Skirt Steak Over Traditional Mediterranean Hummus
Prep time: 10 minutes|Cook time:10 minutes|Serves 4

- 1 pound skirt steak
- 1 teaspoon salt
- ½ teaspoon freshly ground black pepper
- 2 cups prepared hummus (see Creamy Traditional Hummus)
- 1 tablespoon extra-virgin olive oil
- ½ cup pine nuts

1. Preheat a grill, grill pan, or lightly oiled frying pan to medium heat.
2. Season both sides of the steak with salt and pepper.
3. Cook the meat on each side for 3 to 5 minutes; 3 minutes for medium, and 5 minutes on each side

for well done. Let the meat rest for 5 minutes.
4. Rasher the meat into thin strips.
5. Spread the hummus on a serving dish, and evenly distribute the beef on top of the hummus.
6. In a small saucepan, over low heat, add the olive oil and pine nuts. Toast them for 3 minutes, constantly stirring them with a spoon so that they don't burn.
7. Spoon the pine nuts over the beef and serve.

Pressure Cooker Moroccan Pot Roast
Prep time: 15 minutes|Cook time:50 minutes|Serves 4

- 8 ounces mushrooms, rasherd
- 4 tablespoons extra-virgin olive oil
- 3 small onions, cut into 2-inch pieces
- 2 tablespoons paprika
- 1½ tablespoons garam masala
- 2 teaspoons salt
- ¼ teaspoon ground white pepper
- 2 tablespoons tomato paste
- 1 small Aubergine, peeled and diced
- 1¼ cups low-sodium beef broth
- ½ cup halved apricots
- ⅓ cup golden sultanas
- 3 pounds beef chuck roast
- 2 tablespoons honey
- 1 tablespoon dried mint
- 2 cups cooked brown rice

1. Set an electric pressure cooker to Sauté and put the mushrooms and oil in the cooker.
2. Sauté for 5 minutes, then add the onions, paprika, garam masala, salt, and white pepper.
3. Stir in the tomato paste and continue to sauté.
4. Add the Aubergine and sauté for 5 more minutes, until softened.
5. Pour in the broth. Add the apricots and sultanas. Sear the meat for 2 minutes on each side.
6. Close and lock the lid and set the pressure cooker to high for 50 minutes.
7. When cooking is complete, quick release the pressure.
8. Carefully remove the lid, then remove the meat from the sauce and break it into pieces.
9. While the meat is removed, stir honey and mint into the sauce.
10. Assemble plates with ½ cup of brown rice, ½ cup of pot roast sauce, and 3 to 5 pieces of pot roast.

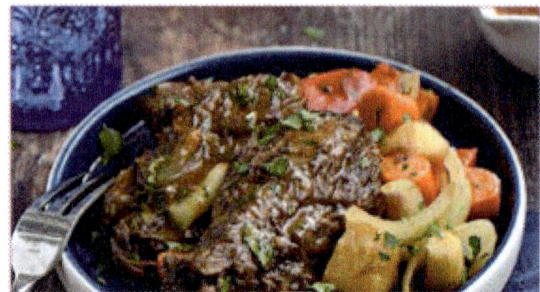

Skirt steak with Artichokes

Prep time: 15 minutes|Cook time:60 minutes|Serves 4 to 6

- 4 tablespoons grapeseed oil, divided
- 2 pounds skirt steak
- 1 (14-ounce) can artichoke hearts, drained and roughly chopped
- 1 onion, diced
- 8 garlic cloves, chopped
- 1 (32-ounce) container low-sodium beef broth
- 1 (14.5-ounce) can diced tomatoes, drained
- 1 cup tomato sauce
- 2 tablespoons tomato paste
- 1 teaspoon dried oregano
- 1 teaspoon dried parsley
- 1 teaspoon dried basil
- ½ teaspoon ground cumin
- 3 bay leaves
- 2 to 3 cups cooked couscous (optional)

1. Preheat the oven to 220°F.
2. In an oven-safe sauté pan or frying pan, heat 3 tablespoons of oil on medium heat.
3. Sear the steak for 2 minutes per side on both sides.
4. Transfer the steak to the oven for 30 minutes, or until desired tenderness.
5. Meanwhile, in a large pot, combine the remaining 1 tablespoon of oil, artichoke hearts, onion, and garlic. Pour in the beef broth, tomatoes, tomato sauce, and tomato paste.
6. Stir in oregano, parsley, basil, cumin, and bay leaves.
7. Cook the vegetables, covered, for 30 minutes.
8. Remove bay leaf and serve with skirt steak and ½ cup of couscous per plate, if using.

Spanish Pepper Steak

Prep time: 10 minutes|Cook time:20 minutes|Serves 4

- 1 pound beef fillet
- 1 tablespoon smoked paprika
- ¼ cup extra-virgin olive oil
- 3 tablespoons garlic, minced
- 1½ teaspoons salt
- 1 large onion, rasherd
- 2 large capsicums, any color, rasherd

1. Cut the beef into thin strips. Season with paprika.
2. In a large frying pan over medium heat, cook the olive oil, garlic, beef, and salt for 7 minutes, using tongs to toss.
3. Turn the heat to low and add in the onion. Cook for 7 minutes.
4. Add the capsicums and cook for 6 minutes.

Pan-Fried Pork Cutlets with Peppers and Onions

Prep time: 5 minutes|Cook time:25 minutes|Serves 4

- 4 (4-ounce) pork cutlets, untrimmed
- 1½ teaspoons salt, divided
- 1 teaspoon freshly ground black pepper, divided
- ½ cup extra-virgin olive oil, divided
- 1 red or orange bell pepper, thinly rasherd
- 1 green bell pepper, thinly rasherd
- 1 small yellow onion, thinly rasherd
- 2 teaspoons dried Italian herbs (such as oregano, parsley, or rosemary)
- 2 garlic cloves, minced
- 1 tablespoon balsamic vinegar

1. Season the pork cutlets with 1 teaspoon salt and ½ teaspoon pepper.
2. In a large frying pan, heat ¼ cup olive oil over medium-high heat.
3. Fry the pork cutlets in the oil until browned and almost cooked through but not fully cooked, 4 to 5 minutes per side, depending on the thickness of cutlets.
4. Remove from the frying pan and cover to keep warm.
5. Pour the remaining ¼ cup olive oil in the frying pan and sauté the rasherd peppers, onions, and herbs over medium-high heat until tender, 6 to 8 minutes.
6. Add the garlic, stirring to combine, and return the pork to frying pan. Cover, reduce the heat to low, and cook for another 2 to 3 minutes, or until the pork is cooked through.
7. Turn off the heat. Using a slotted spoon, transfer the pork, peppers, and onions to a serving platter.
8. Add the vinegar to the oil in the frying pan and whisk to combine well.
9. Drizzle the vinaigrette over the pork and serve warm.

Beef Stew with Green Peas

Prep time: 5 minutes|Cook time:10 minutes|Serves 4

- 2 lb beef, tender cuts, boneless, cut into bits
- 2 cups green peas
- 1 onion, diced
- 1 tomato, diced
- 3 cups beef broth
- ½ cup tomato paste
- 1 tsp cayenne pepper, ground
- 1 tbsp flour
- 1 tsp salt
- ½ tsp dried thyme, ground
- ½ tsp red pepper flakes

1. Add all ingredients in the instant pot.
2. Seal the lid, press Manual/Pressure Cook and cook for 10 minutes on High Pressure.
3. When done, release the steam naturally, for 10 minutes and serve.

Moroccan Stuffed Peppers

Prep time: 10 minutes|Cook time:30 minutes|Serves 4

- ¼ cup, plus 2 tablespoons extra-virgin olive oil, divided
- 2 large red capsicums
- 1 pound minced beef
- 1 small onion, finely chopped
- 2 garlic cloves, minced
- 2 tablespoons chopped fresh sage or 2 teaspoons dried sage
- 1 teaspoon salt
- 1 teaspoon ground allspice
- ½ teaspoon freshly ground black pepper
- ½ cup chopped fresh flat-leaf Italian parsley
- ½ cup chopped baby rocket leaves
- ½ cup chopped walnuts
- 1 tablespoon freshly squeezed orange juice

1. Preheat the oven to 215 .
2. Drizzle 1 tablespoon olive oil in a rimmed baking tray and swirl to coat the bottom.
3. Remove the stems from the peppers and cut in half lengthwise, then remove the seeds and membranes.
4. Place cut-side down on the prepared baking tray and roast until just softened, 5 to 8 minutes.
5. Remove from the oven and allow to cool.
6. Meanwhile, in a large frying pan, heat 1 tablespoon olive oil over medium-high heat.
7. Add the beef and onions and sauté until the meat is browned and cooked through, 8 to 10 minutes.
8. Add the garlic, sage, salt, allspice, and pepper and sauté for 2 more minutes.
9. Remove from the heat and cool slightly.
10. Stir in the parsley, rocket , walnuts, orange juice, and remaining ¼ cup olive oil and mix well.
11. Stuff the filling into each pepper half. Return to the oven and cook for 5 minutes.
12. Serve warm.

Baked Lamb Kofta Meatballs

Prep time: 15 minutes|Cook time:30 minutes|Serves 4

- ¼ cup walnuts
- ½ small onion
- 1 garlic clove
- 1 roasted piquillo pepper
- 2 tablespoons fresh parsley
- 2 tablespoons fresh mint
- ¼ teaspoon salt
- ¼ teaspoon cumin
- ¼ teaspoon allspice
- Pinch cayenne pepper
- 8 ounces lean ground lamb

1. Preheat the oven to 170 and set the rack to the middle position. Line a baking tray with foil.
2. In the bowl of a food processor, combine the walnuts, onion, garlic, roasted pepper, parsley, mint, salt, cumin, allspice, and cayenne pepper.

Pulse about 10 times to combine everything.
3. Transfer the spice mixture to the bowl and add the lamb. With your hands or a spatula, mix the spices into the lamb.
4. Roll into 1½-inch balls (about the size of golf balls).
5. Place the meatballs on the foil-lined baking tray and bake for 30 minutes, or until cooked to an internal temperature of 80 .

Roast Pork Tenderlon With Cherry-Balsamic Sauce

Prep time: 20 minutes|Cook time:20 minutes|Serves 4

- 1 cup frozen cherries, thawed
- ⅓ cup balsamic vinegar
- 1 fresh rosemary sprig
- 1 (8-ounce) pork fillet
- ¼ teaspoon salt
- ⅛ teaspoon freshly ground black pepper
- 1 tablespoon olive oil

1. Combine the cherries and vinegar in a liquidiser and purée until smooth.
2. Pour into a saucepan, add the rosemary sprig, and bring the mixture to a boil.
3. Reduce the heat to medium-low and simmer for 15 minutes, or until it's reduced by half.
4. While the sauce is simmering, preheat the oven to 215 and set the rack in the middle position.
5. Season the pork on all sides with the salt and pepper.
6. Heat the oil in a sauté pan over medium-high heat. Add the pork and sear for 3 minutes, turning often, until it's golden on all sides.
7. Transfer the pork to an oven-safe baking dish and roast for 15 minutes, or until the internal temperature is 75 .
8. Let the pork rest for 5 minutes before serving.
9. Serve rasherd and topped with the cherry-balsamic sauce.

Pork Cutlets with Baby Carrots

Prep time: 5 minutes|Cook time:25 minutes|Serves 4

- 1 pound Pork Cutlets
- 1 pound Baby Carrots
- 1 Onion, rasherd
- 1 tbsp Butter
- 1 cup Vegetable Broth
- 1 tsp Garlic Powder
- Salt and Black Pepper, to taste

1. Season the pork with salt and pepper.
2. Melt butter on SAUTÉ, and brown the pork on all sides.
3. Stir in carrots and onions and cook for 2 more minutes, until soft.
4. Pour in the broth, and add garlic powder. Season with salt and pepper.
5. Seal the lid and cook for 20 minutes on MEAT/STEW mode at High.
6. When ready, release the pressure quickly.

Potato Chowder with Hot Prawn

Prep time: 5 minutes|Cook time:15 minutes|Serves 4

- 4 rashers pancetta, chopped
- 4 tbsp minced garlic
- 1 onion, chopped
- 2 potatoes, chopped
- 16 ounces Tinned corn kernels
- 4 cups vegetable stock
- 1 tsp dried rosemary
- 1 tsp salt
- 1 tsp black pepper
- 1 pound king prawns, peeled, deveined
- 1 tbsp olive oil
- ½ tsp red Chili con carne flakes
- ¾ cup heavy cream

1. Fry the pancetta for 5 minutes until crispy, on Sauté mode, and set aside.
2. Add in 2 tbsp of garlic and onion, and stir-fry for 3 minutes.
3. Add in potatoes, corn, stock, rosemary, half of the salt, and pepper.
4. Seal the lid and cook on High Pressure for 10 minutes.
5. Do a quick Pressure release.
6. Remove to a serving bowl. In a bowl, toss the Prawn in the remaining garlic, salt, black pepper, olive oil, and flakes.
7. Wipe the pot clean and fry Prawn for 3-4 minutes per side, until pink.
8. Mix in the heavy cream and cook for 2 minutes.
9. Add Prawn to chowder, garnish with the reserved pancetta and serve immediately.

Italian Salmon with Creamy Polenta

Prep time: 5 minutes|Cook time:15 minutes|Serves 4

- 1 cup corn Semolina polenta
- ½ cup milk
- 3 cups chicken stock
- 3 tbsp butter
- Salt to taste
- 3 tbsp Italian seasoning
- 1 tbsp sugar
- 4 salmon fillets, skin removed
- Cooking spray

1. Combine polenta, milk, chicken stock, butter, and salt in the pot. Stir and bring mixture to boil on Sauté.
2. In a bowl mix Italian seasoning, sugar, and salt.
3. Oil the fillets with cooking spray and add the spice mixture.
4. Insert a trivet and arrange the fillets on top.
5. Seal the lid and cook on High Pressure for 9 minutes.
6. Do a natural pressure release for 10 minutes.
7. Stir and serve immediately with the salmon.

Crabmeat with Asparagus & Broccoli Pilaf

Prep time: 5 minutes|Cook time:15 minutes|Serves 4

- ½ pound asparagus, trimmed and cut into 1-inch pieces
- ½ pound broccoli florets
- Salt to taste
- 2 tbsp olive oil
- 1 small onion, chopped (about ½ cup)
- 1 cup rice
- ⅓ cup white wine
- 3 cups vegetable stock
- 8 ounces lump crabmeat

1. Heat oil on Sauté and cook onions for 3 minutes, until soft. Stir in rice and cook for 1 minute.
2. Pour in the wine. Cook for 2 to 3 minutes, stirring, until the liquid has almost evaporated.
3. Add vegetable stock and salt; stir to combine. Place a trivet atop.
4. Arrange the broccoli and asparagus on the trivet.
5. Seal the lid and cook on High Pressure for 8 minutes. Do a quick release.
6. Remove the vegetables to a bowl.
7. Fluff the rice with a fork and add in the crabmeat, heat for a minute.
8. Taste and adjust the seasoning.
9. Serve immediately topped with broccoli and asparagus.

Orange Salmon Fillets

Prep time: 5 minutes|Cook time:12 minutes|Serves 3

- 1 lb salmon filets
- 1 cup orange juice, freshly squeezed
- 2 tbsp cornflour
- 1 tsp himalayan pink salt
- ½ tsp black pepper, freshly ground
- ½ tsp garlic, minced
- 1 tsp orange zest, freshly grated

1. Add all ingredients and seal the lid. Cook on High pressure for 10 minutes.
2. Do a quick pressure release.

Garlic-Lemon Salmon Steak

Prep time: 5 minutes|Cook time:60 minutes|Serves 3

- 1 lb salmon steaks
- 1 tsp garlic powder
- ½ tsp rosemary powder
- 1 cup olive oil
- ½ cup apple cider vinegar
- 1 tsp salt
- ¼ cup lemon juice
- ½ tsp white pepper

1. In a bowl, mix garlic, rosemary, olive oil, apple cider vinegar, salt, lemon juice, and pepper.
2. Pour the mixture into a Ziploc bag along with the salmon.
3. Seal the bag and shake to coat well. Refrigerate for 30 minutes.
4. Pour in 3 cups of water in the instant pot and insert the trivet.
5. Remove the fish from the Ziploc bag and place on top.
6. Reserve the marinade.
7. Seal lid and cook on Steam mode for 15 minutes on High Pressure.
8. When ready, do a quick release and remove the steaks.
9. Discard the liquid and wipe clean the pot. Grease with some of the marinade and hit Sauté.
10. Add salmon steaks and brown on both sides for 3-4 minutes.

Lemon Pepper Prawn in Air Fryer

Prep time: 5 minutes|Cook time:10 minutes|Serves 4

- Green Prawn: 1 and 1/2 cup peeled, deveined
- Olive oil: 1/2 tablespoon
- Garlic powder: ¼ tsp
- Lemon pepper: 1 tsp
- Paprika: ¼ tsp
- Juice of one lemon

1. Preheat the Air Fryer to 200 .
2. In a bowl, mix lemon pepper, olive oil, paprika, garlic powder, and lemon juice. Mix well. Add Prawns and coat well.
3. Add Prawns to the Air Fryer, and cook for 8 minutes.
4. Top with lemon rashers before serving.

Lemon Garlic Prawn in Air Fryer

Prep time: 5 minutes|Cook time:10 minutes|Serves 2

- Olive oil: 1 Tbsp.
- Small Prawn: 4 cups, peeled, tails removed
- One lemon juice and zest
- Parsley: 1/4 cup rasherd
- Red pepper flakes (crushed): 1 pinch
- Four cloves of grated garlic
- Sea salt: 1/4 teaspoon

1. Preheat the Air Fryer to 200 .
2. Mix olive oil, lemon zest, red pepper flakes, Prawn, flaked salt , and garlic in a bowl and coat the Prawn well.
3. Place Prawn in the Air Fryer basket and coat with oil spray.
4. Cook at 200 for 8 minutes.
5. Toss the Prawn halfway through.
6. Serve with lemon rashers and parsley.

Parmesan Prawn

Prep time: 5 minutes|Cook time:10 minutes|Serves 4

- Olive oil: 2 tablespoons
- Jumbo cooked Prawn: 8 cups, peeled, deveined
- Parmesan cheese: 2/3 cup (grated)
- Onion powder: 1 teaspoon
- Pepper: 1 teaspoon
- Four cloves of minced garlic
- Oregano: 1/2 teaspoon
- Basil: 1 teaspoon
- Lemon wedges

1. Mix parmesan cheese, onion powder, oregano, olive oil, garlic, basil, and pepper in a bowl.
2. Coat the Prawn in this mixture.
3. Spray oil on the Air Fryer basket and put Prawn in it.
4. Cook for ten minutes at 180 .
5. Drizzle the lemon on the Prawn before serving.

Juicy Air Fryer Salmon

Prep time: 5 minutes|Cook time:12 minutes|Serves 4

- Lemon pepper seasoning: 2 teaspoons
- Salmon: 4 cups
- Olive oil: one tablespoon
- Seafood seasoning: 2 teaspoons
- Half lemon's juice
- Garlic powder: 1 teaspoon
- Salt to taste

1. In a bowl, add one tbsp. of olive oil and half lemon juice.
2. Pour this mixture over salmon and rub. Leave the skin on salmon.
3. It will come off when cooked.
4. Rub the salmon with salt and spices.
5. Put greaseproof paper in the air fryer basket.
6. Put the salmon in the Air Fryer.
7. Cook at 180 for ten minutes.
8. Cook until inner salmon temperature reaches 70 .
9. Let the salmon rest five minutes before serving.
10. Serve with lemon wedges.

Steamed Mussels in White Wine Sauce

Prep time: 5 minutes|Cook time:10 minutes|Serves 4

- 2 pounds small mussels
- 1 tablespoon extra-virgin olive oil
- 1 cup thinly rasherd red onion (about ½ medium onion)
- 3 garlic cloves, rasherd (about 1½ teaspoons)
- 1 cup dry white wine
- 2 (¼-inch-thick) lemon rashers
- ¼ teaspoon freshly ground black pepper
- ¼ teaspoon kosher or sea salt
- Fresh lemon wedges, for serving (optional)

1. In a large colander in the sink, run cold water over the mussels (but don't let the mussels sit in standing water).
2. Leave the mussels in the colander until you're ready to use them.
3. In a large frying pan over medium-high heat, heat the oil.
4. Add the onion and cook for 4 minutes, stirring occasionally.
5. Add the garlic and cook for 1 minute, stirring constantly. Add the wine, lemon rashers, pepper, and salt, and bring to a simmer.
6. Cook for 2 minutes.
7. Add the mussels and cover. Cook for 3 minutes, or until the mussels open their shells.
8. Gently shake the pan two or three times while they are cooking.
9. All the shells should now be wide open.
10. Using a slotted spoon, discard any mussels that are still closed.
11. Spoon the opened mussels into a shallow serving bowl, and pour the broth over the top.
12. Serve with additional fresh lemon rashers, if desired.

Orange and Garlic Prawn

Prep time: 20 minutes|Cook time:10 minutes|Serves 6

- 1 large orange
- 3 tablespoons extra-virgin olive oil, divided
- 1 tablespoon chopped fresh rosemary (about 3 sprigs) or 1 teaspoon dried rosemary
- 1 tablespoon chopped fresh thyme (about 6 sprigs) or 1 teaspoon dried thyme
- 3 garlic cloves, minced (about 1½ teaspoons)
- ¼ teaspoon freshly ground black pepper
- ¼ teaspoon kosher or sea salt
- 1½ pounds fresh green Prawn, (or frozen and thawed green Prawn) shells and tails removed

1. Zest the entire orange using a Microplane or citrus grater.
2. In a large zip-top plastic bag, combine the orange zest and 2 tablespoons of oil with the rosemary, thyme, garlic, pepper, and salt.
3. Add the Prawn, seal the bag, and gently massage the Prawn until all the ingredients are combined and the Prawn is completely covered with the seasonings. Set aside.
4. Heat a grill, grill pan, or a large frying pan over medium heat.
5. Brush on or swirl in the remaining 1 tablespoon of oil.
6. Add half the Prawn, and cook for 4 to 6 minutes, or until the Prawn turn pink and white, flipping halfway through if on the grill or stirring every minute if in a pan.
7. Transfer the Prawn to a large serving bowl.
8. Repeat with the remaining Prawn, and add them to the bowl.
9. While the Prawn cook, peel the orange and cut the flesh into bite-size pieces.
10. Add to the serving bowl, and toss with the cooked Prawn. Serve immediately or refrigerate and serve cold.

Paprika-Spiced Fish

Prep time: 5 minutes|Cook time:10 minutes|Serves 4

- 4 (5-ounce) sea bass fillets
- ½ teaspoon salt
- 1 tablespoon smoked paprika
- 3 tablespoons unsalted butter
- Lemon wedges

1. Season the fish on both sides with the salt.
2. Repeat with the paprika.
3. Preheat a frying pan over high heat. Melt the butter.
4. Once the butter is melted, add the fish and cook for 4 minutes on each side.
5. Once the fish is done cooking, move to a serving dish and squeeze lemon over the top.

Baked Jewfish with Cherry Tomatoes
Prep time: 5 minutes|Cook time:15 minutes|Serves 4

- 4 (5-ounce) pieces of boneless jewfish, skin on
- 1 pint (2 cups) cherry tomatoes
- 3 tablespoons garlic, minced
- ¼ cup extra-virgin olive oil
- 1 teaspoon salt

1. Preheat the oven to 225 .
2. Put the jewfish in a large baking dish; place the tomatoes around the jewfish.
3. In a small bowl, combine the garlic, lemon juice, olive oil, and salt.
4. Pour the sauce over the jewfish and tomatoes.
5. Put the baking dish in the oven and bake for 15 minutes.
6. Serve immediately.

Herbed Prawn Pita
Prep time: 5 minutes|Cook time:8 minutes|Serves 4

- 1 pound medium Prawn, peeled and deveined
- 2 tablespoons olive oil
- 1 teaspoon dried oregano
- ½ teaspoon dried thyme
- ½ teaspoon garlic powder
- ¼ teaspoon onion powder
- ½ teaspoon salt
- ¼ teaspoon black pepper
- 4 whole wheat pitas
- 4 ounces feta cheese, crumbled
- 1 cup shredded lettuce
- 1 tomato, diced
- ¼ cup black olives, rasherd
- 1 lemon

1. Preheat the oven to 190 .
2. In a medium bowl, combine the Prawn with the olive oil, oregano, thyme, garlic powder, onion powder, salt, and black pepper.
3. Pour Prawn in a single layer in the air fryer basket and cook for 6 to 8 minutes, or until cooked through.
4. Remove from the air fryer and divide into warmed pitas with feta, lettuce, tomato, olives, and a squeeze of lemon.

Crushed Marcona Almond Swordfish
Prep time: 25 minutes|Cook time:15 minutes|Serves 4

- ½ cup almond flour
- ¼ cup crushed Marcona almonds
- ½ to 1 teaspoon salt, divided
- 2 pounds Swordfish, preferably 1 inch thick
- 1 large egg, beaten (optional)
- ¼ cup pure apple cider
- ¼ cup extra-virgin olive oil, plus more for frying
- 3 to 4 sprigs flat-leaf parsley, chopped

- 1 lemon, juiced
- 1 tablespoon Spanish paprika
- 5 medium baby portobello mushrooms, chopped (optional)
- 4 or 5 chopped spring onions, both green and white parts
- 3 to 4 garlic cloves, peeled
- ¼ cup chopped pitted kalamata olives

1. On a dinner plate, spread the flour and crushed Marcona almonds and mix in the salt.
2. Alternately, pour the flour, almonds, and ¼ teaspoon of salt into a large plastic food storage bag.
3. Add the fish and coat it with the flour mixture.
4. If a thicker coat is desired, repeat this step after dipping the fish in the egg (if using).
5. In a measuring cup, combine the apple cider, ¼ cup of olive oil, parsley, lemon juice, paprika, and ¼ teaspoon of salt. Mix well and set aside.
6. Once the oil is hot, add the fish and brown for 3 to 5 minutes, then turn the fish over and add the mushrooms (If using), spring onions, garlic, and olives.
7. Cook for an additional 3 minutes.
8. Once the other side of the fish is brown, remove the fish from the pan and set aside.
9. Pour the cider mixture into the frying pan and mix well with the vegetables.
10. Put the fried fish into the frying pan on top of the mixture and cook with sauce on medium-low heat for 10 minutes, until the fish flakes easily with a fork.
11. Carefully remove the fish from the pan and plate.
12. Spoon the sauce over the fish. Serve with white rice or home-fried potatoes.

Greek Stuffed Squid
Prep time: 15 minutes|Cook time:30 minutes|Serves 4

- 8 ounces frozen spinach, thawed and drained (about 1½ cup)
- 4 ounces crumbled goat cheese
- ½ cup chopped pitted olives (I like Kalamata in this recipe)
- ½ cup extra-virgin olive oil, divided
- ¼ cup chopped sun-dried tomatoes
- ¼ cup chopped fresh flat-leaf Italian parsley
- 2 garlic cloves, finely minced
- ¼ teaspoon freshly ground black pepper
- 2 pounds baby squid, cleaned and tentacles removed

1. Preheat the oven to 175 .
2. In a medium bowl, combine the spinach, goat cheese, olives, ¼ cup olive oil, sun-dried tomatoes, parsley, garlic, and pepper.
3. Pour 2 tablespoons olive oil in the bottom of an 8-inch square baking dish and spread to coat the bottom.
4. Stuff each cleaned squid with 2 to 3 tablespoons of the cheese mixture, depending on the size of squid, and place in the prepared baking dish.
5. Drizzle the tops with the remaining 2 tablespoons olive oil and bake until the squid are cooked through, 25 to 30 minutes.
6. Remove from the oven and allow to cool 5 to 10 minutes before serving.

Chapter 10
Vegetarian Recipes

Vegetarian Paella

Prep time: 5 minutes|Cook time:25 minutes|Serves 4

- ½ cup frozen green peas
- 2 carrots, finely chopped
- 1 cup fire-roasted tomatoes
- 1 cup Courgette, finely chopped
- ½ tbsp celery root, finely chopped
- 6 saffron threads
- 1 tbsp turmeric, ground
- 1 tsp salt
- ½ tsp freshly ground black pepper
- 2 cup vegetable broth
- 1 cup long grain rice

1. Place all ingredients, except rice, in the instant pot.
2. Stir well and seal the lid. Cook on Rice mode for 8 minutes, on High.
3. Do a quick release, open the lid and stir in the rice.
4. Seal the lid and cook on High pressure for 3 minutes.
5. When ready, release the pressure naturally, for about 10 minutes.

Vegetable Stew

Prep time: 5 minutes|Cook time:50 minutes|Serves 4

- 1 lb potatoes, peeled, cut into bite-sized pieces
- 2 carrots, peeled, chopped
- 3 celery stalks, chopped
- 2 onions, peeled, chopped
- 1 Courgette, cut into ½ -inch thick rashers
- A handful of fresh celery leaves
- 2 tbsp butter, unsalted
- 3 tbsp olive oil
- 2 cups vegetable broth
- 1 tbsp paprika
- 1 tbsp salt
- 1 tsp black pepper

1. Warm oil on Sauté and stir-fry the onions for 3-4 minutes, until translucent.
2. Add carrots, celery, Courgette, and ¼ cup of broth.
3. Continue to cook for 10 more minutes, stirring constantly.
4. Stir in potatoes, cayenne pepper, salt, pepper, bay leaves, remaining broth, and celery leaves.
5. Seal the lid and cook on Meat/Stew mode for 30 minutes on High.
6. Do a quick release and stir in 2 tbsp of butter.

Stewed Kidney Bean

Prep time: 5 minutes|Cook time:25 minutes|Serves 4

- 6 oz red beans, cooked
- 2 carrots, chopped
- 2 celery stalks, cut into pieces
- 1 onion, peeled, chopped
- 2 tbsp tomato paste
- 1 bay leaf
- 2 cups vegetable broth
- 3 tbsp olive oil
- 1 tsp salt
- A handful of fresh parsley

1. Warm oil on Sauté and stir-fry the onions, for 3 minutes, until soft.
2. Add celery and carrots.
3. Cook for 5 more minutes, adding 1 tbsp of broth at the time.
4. Add red beans, bay leaf, salt, parsley, and tomato paste.
5. Stir in 1 tbsp of flour and pour in the remaining broth.
6. Seal the lid and cook on High pressure for 5 minutes on.
7. Do a natural release, for about 10 minutes.
8. Sprinkle with some fresh parsley and serve warm.

Lentil Spread with Parmesan

Prep time: 5 minutes|Cook time:10 minutes|Serves 6

- 1 lb of lentils, cooked
- 1 cup sweet corn
- 2 tomatoes, diced
- 3 tbsp tomato paste
- ½ tsp dried oregano, ground
- 2 tbsp Parmesan Cheese
- 1 tsp salt
- ½ tsp red pepper flakes
- 3 tbsp olive oil
- 1 cup water
- ¼ cup red wine

1. Heat oil on Sauté and add tomatoes, tomato paste, and ½ cup of water. Sprinkle with salt and oregano and stir-fry for 5 minutes.
2. Press Cancel and add lentils, sweet corn, and wine.
3. Pour in the remaining water and seal the lid. Cook on High Pressure for 2 minutes.
4. Do a quick release. Set aside to cool completely and refrigerate for 30 minutes.
5. Sprinkle with Parmesan Cheese before serving.

Broccoli & Orecchiette Pasta with Feta
Prep time: 5 minutes|Cook time:20 minutes|Serves 4

- 1 (9 oz) pack orecchiette
- 16 oz broccoli, roughly chopped
- 2 garlic cloves
- 3 tbsp olive oil
- 1 tbsp grated feta
- 1 tsp salt
- ¼ tsp black pepper

1. Place the orecchiette and broccoli in your instant pot. Cover with water and seal the lid.
2. Cook on High Pressure for 10 minutes. Do a quick release.
3. Drain the broccoli and orecchiette. Set aside.
4. Heat the olive oil on Sauté mode.
5. Stir-fry garlic for 2 minutes. Stir in broccoli, orecchiette, salt, and pepper.
6. Cook for 2 more minutes.
7. Press Cancel and stir in grated feta, to serve.

Basil Tomatoes
Prep time: 10 minutes|Cook time:10 minutes|Serves 2

- Three tomatoes, halved
- One tablespoon fresh basil, chopped
- Olive oil cook spray
- Salt and ground black pepper

1. Drizzle cut sides of the tomato halves with cook spray evenly.
2. Sprinkle with pepper, salt, and basil.
3. Select the "Air Fry" mode of the Air Fryer and set the cooking time to ten minutes.
4. Set the temperature to 160 .
5. Arrange the tomatoes in Air Fryer Basket and cook them.

Cheesy Spinach
Prep time: 10 minutes|Cook time:15 minutes|Serves 3

- 1 (10-ounce) package frozen spinach, thawed
- ½ cup onion, chopped
- Four ounces cream cheese, chopped
- ¼ cup Parmesan cheese, shredded
- Two teaspoons garlic, minced
- ½ teaspoon ground nutmeg
- Salt and pepper

1. In a bowl, mix well spinach, garlic, cream cheese, onion, nutmeg, salt, and pepper.
2. Place spinach mixture into a baking pan.
3. Preheat the Air Fryer and arrange the baking pan in the basket.
4. Select "Air Fry" mode and set the temperature at 170 .
5. Cook for ten minutes.

Grilled Stuffed Portabello Mushrooms
Prep time: 5 minutes|Cook time:25 minutes|Serves 6

- 3 tablespoons extra-virgin olive oil, divided
- 1 cup diced onion (about ½ medium onion)
- 2 garlic cloves, minced (about 1 teaspoon)
- 3 cups chopped mushrooms, any variety
- 1 large or 2 small Courgette or summer squash, diced (about 2 cups)
- 1 cup chopped tomato (about 1 large tomato)
- 1 teaspoon dried oregano
- ¼ teaspoon crushed red pepper
- ¼ teaspoon kosher or sea salt
- 6 large portabello mushrooms, stems and gills removed
- Nonstick cooking spray (if needed)
- 4 ounces fresh mozzarella cheese, shredded
- Additional dried oregano, for serving (optional)

1. In a large frying pan over medium heat, heat 2 tablespoons of oil.
2. Add the onion and cook for 4 minutes, stirring occasionally.
3. Stir in the garlic and cook for 1 minute, stirring often.
4. Stir in the mushrooms, Courgette, tomato, oregano, crushed red pepper, and salt. Cook for 10 minutes, stirring occasionally.
5. Remove from the heat.
6. While the veggies are cooking, heat the grill or grill pan to medium-high heat.
7. Brush the remaining tablespoon of oil over the portabello mushroom caps.
8. Place the mushrooms bottom-side (where the stem was removed) down on the grill or pan.
9. Cover and cook for 5 minutes. (If using a grill pan, cover with a sheet of Aluminium foil sprayed with nonstick cooking spray.)
10. Flip the mushroom caps over, and spoon about ½ cup of the cooked vegetable mixture into each cap.
11. Top each with about 2½ tablespoons of mozzarella and additional oregano, if desired.
12. Cover and grill for 4 to 5 minutes, or until the cheese melts.
13. Remove each portabello with a spatula, and let them sit for about 5 minutes to cool slightly before serving.

Sautéed Garlic Spinach
Prep time: 5 minutes|Cook time:10 minutes|Serves 4

- ¼ cup extra-virgin olive oil
- 1 large onion, thinly rasherd
- 3 cloves garlic, minced
- 6 (1-pound) bags of baby spinach, washed
- ½ teaspoon salt
- 1 lemon, cut into wedges

1. Cook the olive oil, onion, and garlic in a large frying pan for 2 minutes over medium heat.
2. Add one bag of spinach and ½ teaspoon of salt.
3. Cover the frying pan and let the spinach wilt for 30 seconds. Repeat (omitting the salt), adding 1 bag of spinach at a time.
4. Once all the spinach has been added, remove the cover and cook for 3 minutes, letting some of the moisture evaporate.
5. Serve warm with a generous squeeze of lemon over the top.

Garlicky Sautéed Courgette with Mint
Prep time: 5 minutes|Cook time:10 minutes|Serves 4

- 3 large green Courgette
- 3 tablespoons extra-virgin olive oil
- 1 large onion, chopped
- 3 cloves garlic, minced
- 1 teaspoon salt
- 1 teaspoon dried mint

1. Cut the Courgette into ½-inch cubes.
2. In a large frying pan over medium heat, cook the olive oil, onions, and garlic for 3 minutes, stirring constantly.
3. Add the Courgette and salt to the frying pan and toss to combine with the onions and garlic, cooking for 5 minutes.
4. Add the mint to the frying pan, tossing to combine.
5. Cook for another 2 minutes. Serve warm.

Freekeh, Chickpea, and Herb Salad
Prep time: 15 minutes|Cook time:10 minutes|Serves 4 to 6

- 1 (15-ounce) can chickpeas, rinsed and drained
- 1 cup cooked freekeh
- 1 cup thinly rasherd celery
- 1 bunch spring onions, both white and green parts, finely chopped
- ½ cup chopped fresh flat-leaf parsley
- ¼ cup chopped fresh mint
- 3 tablespoons chopped celery leaves
- ½ teaspoon flaked salt
- ⅓ cup extra-virgin olive oil
- ¼ cup freshly squeezed lemon juice
- ¼ teaspoon cumin seeds
- 1 teaspoon garlic powder

1. In a large bowl, combine the chickpeas, freekeh, celery, spring onions, parsley, mint, celery leaves, and salt and toss lightly.
2. In a small bowl, whisk together the olive oil, lemon juice, cumin seeds, and garlic powder.
3. Once combined, add to freekeh salad.

Kate's Warm Mediterranean Farro Bowl
Prep time: 15 minutes|Cook time:10 minutes|Serves 4 to 6

- ⅓ cup extra-virgin olive oil
- ½ cup chopped red bell pepper
- ⅓ cup chopped red onions
- 2 garlic cloves, minced
- 1 cup Courgette, cut in ½-inch rashers
- ½ cup Tinned chickpeas, drained and rinsed
- ½ cup coarsely chopped artichokes
- 3 cups cooked farro
- Salt
- Freshly ground black pepper
- ¼ cup rasherd olives, for serving (optional)
- ½ cup crumbled feta cheese, for serving (optional)
- 2 tablespoons fresh basil, chiffonade, for serving (optional)
- 3 tablespoons balsamic reduction, for serving (optional)

1. In a large sauté pan or frying pan, heat the oil over medium heat and sauté the pepper, onions, and garlic for about 5 minutes, until tender.
2. Add the Courgette, chickpeas, and artichokes, then stir and continue to sauté vegetables, approximately 5 more minutes, until just soft.
3. Stir in the cooked farro, tossing to combine and cooking enough to heat through.
4. Season with salt and pepper and remove from the heat.
5. Transfer the contents of the pan into the serving vessels or bowls.
6. Top with olives, feta, and basil (if using).
7. Drizzle with balsamic reduction (if using) to finish

Citrus French beans with Red Onions
Prep time: 5 minutes|Cook time:10 minutes|Serves 6

- 1 pound fresh French beans, trimmed
- ½ red onion, rasherd
- 2 tablespoons olive oil
- ½ teaspoon salt
- ¼ teaspoon black pepper
- 1 tablespoon lemon juice
- Lemon wedges, for serving

1. Preheat the air fryer to 180 .
2. In a large bowl, toss the French beans, onion, olive oil, salt, pepper, and lemon juice until combined.
3. Pour the mixture into the air fryer and roast for 5 minutes.
4. Stir well and roast for 5 minutes more.
5. Serve with lemon wedges.

Herbed Ricotta Stuffed Mushrooms

Prep time: 10 minutes|Cook time:30 minutes|Serves 4

- 6 tablespoons extra-virgin olive oil, divided
- 4 portobello mushroom caps, cleaned and gills removed
- 1 cup whole-milk ricotta cheese
- ⅓ cup chopped fresh herbs (such as basil, parsley, rosemary, oregano, or thyme)
- 2 garlic cloves, finely minced
- ½ teaspoon salt
- ¼ teaspoon freshly ground black pepper

1. Preheat the oven to 200 .
2. Line a baking tray with parchment or foil and drizzle with 2 tablespoons olive oil, spreading evenly.
3. Place the mushroom caps on the baking tray, gill-side up.
4. In a medium bowl, mix together the ricotta, herbs, 2 tablespoons olive oil, garlic, salt, and pepper.
5. Stuff each mushroom cap with one-quarter of the cheese mixture, pressing down if needed.
6. Drizzle with remaining 2 tablespoons olive oil and bake until golden brown and the mushrooms are soft, 30 to 35 minutes, depending on the size of the mushrooms.

Braised Greens with Olives and Walnuts

Prep time: 5 minutes|Cook time:20 minutes|Serves 4

- 8 cups fresh greens (such as kale, mustard greens, spinach, or chard)
- 2 to 4 garlic cloves, finely minced
- ½ cup roughly chopped pitted green or black olives
- ½ cup roughly chopped shelled walnuts
- ¼ cup extra-virgin olive oil
- 2 tablespoons red wine vinegar
- 1 to 2 teaspoons freshly chopped herbs such as oregano, basil, rosemary, or thyme

1. Remove the tough stems from the greens and chop into bite-size pieces.
2. Place in a large rimmed frying pan or pot.
3. Turn the heat to high and add the minced garlic and enough water to just cover the greens.
4. Bring to a boil, reduce the heat to low, and simmer until the greens are wilted and tender and most of the liquid has evaporated, adding more if the greens start to burn.
5. For more tender greens such as spinach, this may only take 5 minutes, while tougher greens such as chard may need up to 20 minutes.
6. Once cooked, remove from the heat and add the chopped olives and walnuts.
7. In a small bowl, whisk together olive oil, vinegar, and herbs.
8. Drizzle over the cooked greens and toss to coat. Serve warm.

Crispy Lemon Artichoke Hearts

Prep time: 5 minutes|Cook time:15 minutes|Serves 2

- 1 (15-ounce) can artichoke hearts in water, drained
- 1 egg
- 1 tablespoon water
- ¼ cup whole wheat bread crumbs
- ¼ teaspoon salt
- ¼ teaspoon paprika
- ½ lemon

1. Preheat the air fryer to 190 .
2. In a medium shallow bowl, beat together the egg and water until frothy.
3. In a separate medium shallow bowl, mix together the bread crumbs, salt, and paprika.
4. Dip each artichoke heart into the egg mixture, then into the bread crumb mixture, coating the outside with the crumbs. Place the artichokes hearts in a single layer of the air fryer basket.
5. Fry the artichoke hearts for 15 minutes.
6. Remove the artichokes from the air fryer, and squeeze fresh lemon juice over the top before serving.

Spiced Honey-Walnut Carrots

Prep time: 5 minutes|Cook time:12 minutes|Serves 6

- 1 pound baby carrots
- 2 tablespoons olive oil
- ¼ cup raw honey
- ¼ teaspoon ground cinnamon
- ¼ cup black walnuts, chopped

1. Preheat the air fryer to 180 .
2. In a large bowl, toss the baby carrots with olive oil, honey, and cinnamon until well coated.
3. Pour into the air fryer and roast for 6 minutes.
4. Shake the basket, sprinkle the walnuts on top, and roast for 6 minutes more.
5. Remove the carrots from the air fryer and serve.

Vanilla & Walnut Cake

Prep time: 5 minutes|Cook time:10 minutes|Serves 8

- 3 standard cake crusts
- ½ cup vanilla pudding powder
- ¼ cup caster sugar
- 4 cups milk
- 1 (10.5oz) box chocolate chips
- ¼ cup walnuts, minced

1. Combine vanilla powder, sugar and milk in the inner pot.
2. Cook until the pudding thickens, stirring constantly, on Sauté.
3. Remove from the steel pot.
4. Place one crust onto a springform pan. Pour half of the pudding and sprinkle with minced walnuts and chocolate chips.
5. Cover with another crust and repeat the process. Finish with the final crust and wrap in foil.
6. Insert the trivet, pour in 1 cup of water, and place springform pan on top.
7. Seal the lid and cook for 10 minutes on High Pressure.
8. Do a quick release.
9. Refrigerate overnight.

Vanilla Sweet Tortillas

Prep time: 5 minutes|Cook time:15 minutes|Serves 6

- 2 medium-sized bananas, mashed
- 1¼ cup milk
- 2 eggs
- 1½ cups rolled oats
- 1½ tsp baking powder
- 1 tsp vanilla extract
- 2 tsp coconut oil
- 1 tbsp honey
- ¼ tsp salt
- Non-fat cooking spray

1. Combine the ingredients in a liquidiser and pulse until a completely smooth batter.
2. Grease the inner pot with cooking spray.
3. Spread 1 spoon batter at the bottom.
4. Cook for 2 minutes, on Sauté mode, flip the crepe and cook for another minute.
5. Repeat the process with the remaining batter.
6. Serve immediately.

Pumpkin & Walnut Sweet Rolls

Prep time: 5 minutes|Cook time:25 minutes|Serves 8

- 2 cups pumpkin puree
- 1 tsp vanilla extract
- 2 cups Greek yogurt
- 2 eggs
- 2 tbsp brown sugar
- 2 tbsp unsalted butter, softened
- 2 puff pastry sheets
- 1 cup walnuts, chopped

1. In a bowl, mix yogurt with vanilla essenceuntil completely smooth; set aside.
2. Unfold the pastry and cut each sheet into 4-inch x 7-inch pieces and brush with half of the beaten eggs.
3. Place approximately 2 tbsp of pumpkin puree, and 2 tbsp of the yogurt mixture at the middle of each pastry, sprinkle with walnuts.
4. Fold the sheets and brush with the remaining eggs.
5. Cut the surface with a sharp knife and gently place each strudel into an oiled baking dish.
6. Pour 1 cup of water in the pot and insert the trivet.
7. Place the pan on top.
8. Seal the lid and cook for 25 minutes on High Pressure.
9. Release the pressure naturally, for about 10 minutes.
10. Let it chill for 10 minutes.
11. Carefully Transfer the strudels to a serving plate.

Cinnamon & Lemon Apples

Prep time: 3 minutes|Cook time:10 minutes|Serves 2

- 2 Apples, peeled and cut into wedges
- ½ cup Lemon Juice
- ½ tsp Cinnamon
- 1 tbsp Butter
- 1 cup Water

1. Combine lemon juice and water in the pressure cooker.
2. Place the apple wedges in the steaming basket and lower the basket into the cooker.
3. Seal the lid, select the Pressure Cook for 3 minutes at High.
4. Release the pressure quickly.
5. Open the lid and remove the steaming basket.
6. Transfer the apple wedges to a bowl.Drizzle with almond butter and sprinkle with cinnamon.

Lemon Fool

Prep time: 25 minutes|Cook time:5 minutes|Serves 4

- 1 cup 2% plain Greek yogurt
- 1 medium lemon
- ¼ cup cold water
- 1½ teaspoons cornflour
- 3½ tablespoons honey, divided
- ⅔ cup heavy (whipping) cream
- Fresh fruit and mint leaves, for serving (optional)

1. Place a large glass bowl and the metal beaters from your electric mixer in the refrigerator to chill.
2. Add the yogurt to a medium glass bowl, and place that bowl in the refrigerator to chill as well.
3. Using a Microplane or citrus zester, zest the lemon into a medium, microwave-safe bowl. Halve the lemon, and squeeze 1 tablespoon of lemon juice into the bowl.
4. Add the water and cornflour, and stir well. Whisk in 3 tablespoons of honey.
5. Microwave the lemon mixture on high for 1 minute; stir and microwave for an additional 10 to 30 seconds, until the mixture is thick and bubbling.
6. Remove the bowl of yogurt from the refrigerator, and whisk in the warm lemon mixture.
7. Place the yogurt back in the refrigerator.
8. Remove the large chilled bowl and the beaters from the refrigerator.
9. Assemble your electric mixer with the chilled beaters.
10. Pour the cream into the chilled bowl, and beat until soft peaks form—1 to 3 minutes, depending on the freshness of your cream.
11. Take the chilled yogurt mixture out of the refrigerator.
12. Gently fold it into the whipped cream using a rubber scraper; lift and turn the mixture to prevent the cream from deflating.
13. Chill until serving, at least 15 minutes but no longer than 1 hour.
14. To serve, spoon the lemon fool into four glasses or dessert dishes and drizzle with the remaining ½ tablespoon of honey.
15. Top with fresh fruit and mint, if desired.

Roasted Orange Rice Pudding

Prep time: 10 minutes|Cook time:20 minutes|Serves 6

- Nonstick cooking spray
- 2 medium oranges
- 2 teaspoons extra-virgin olive oil
- ⅛ teaspoon kosher or sea salt
- 2 large eggs, beaten
- 2 cups 2% milk
- 1 cup 100% orange juice
- 1 cup uncooked instant brown rice
- ¼ cup honey
- ½ teaspoon ground cinnamon
- 1 teaspoon vanilla extract

1. Preheat the oven to 220 .
2. Spray a large, rimmed baking tray with nonstick cooking spray. Set aside.
3. Rasher the unpeeled oranges into ¼-inch rounds. Brush with oil, and sprinkle with salt.
4. Place the rashers on the baking tray and roast for 4 minutes. Flip the rashers and roast for 4 more minutes, until they begin to brown. Remove from the oven and set aside.
5. Crack the eggs into a medium bowl near the stove.
6. In a medium saucepan, mix together the milk, orange juice, rice, honey, and cinnamon.
7. Bring to a boil over medium-high heat, stirring constantly.
8. Reduce the heat to medium-low and simmer for 10 minutes, stirring occasionally.
9. Using a measuring cup, scoop out ½ cup of the hot rice mixture and whisk it into the eggs.
10. Then, while constantly stirring the mixture in the pan, slowly pour the egg mixture back into the saucepan (to prevent the eggs from scrambling).
11. Cook on low heat for 1 to 2 minutes, until thickened, stirring constantly; do not boil.
12. Remove from the heat and stir in the vanilla.
13. Let the pudding stand for a few minutes for the rice to soften. The rice will be cooked but slightly chewy.
14. For softer rice, let stand for another half hour.
15. Serve warm or at room temperature, topped with the roasted oranges.

Baklava and Honey
Prep time: 40 minutes|Cook time:1 hour|Serves 8

- 2 cups very finely chopped walnuts or pecans
- 1 teaspoon cinnamon
- 1 cup (2 sticks) of unsalted butter, melted
- 1 (16-ounce) package phyllo dough, thawed
- 1 (12-ounce) jar honey

1. Preheat the oven to 170 .
2. In a bowl, combine the chopped nuts and cinnamon.
3. Using a brush, butter the sides and bottom of a 9-by-13-inch inch baking dish.
4. Remove the phyllo dough from the package and cut it to the size of the baking dish using a sharp knife.
5. Place one sheet of phyllo dough on the bottom of the dish, brush with butter, and repeat until you have 8 layers.
6. Sprinkle ⅓ cup of the nut mixture over the phyllo layers. Top with a sheet of phyllo dough, butter that sheet, and repeat until you have 4 sheets of buttered phyllo dough.
7. Sprinkle ⅓ cup of the nut mixture for another layer of nuts. Repeat the layering of nuts and 4 sheets of buttered phyllo until all the nut mixture is gone. The last layer should be 8 buttered sheets of phyllo.
8. Before you bake, cut the baklava into desired shapes; traditionally this is diamonds, triangles, or squares.
9. Bake the baklava for 1 hour or until the top layer is golden brown.
10. While the baklava is baking, heat the honey in a pan just until it is warm and easy to pour.
11. Once the baklava is done baking, immediately pour the honey evenly over the baklava and let it absorb it, about 20 minutes.
12. Serve warm or at room temperature.

Date and Nut Balls
Prep time: 10 minutes|Cook time:10 minutes|Serves 6 to 8

- 1 cup walnuts or pistachios
- 1 cup unsweetened desiccated coconut
- 14 medjool dates, pits removed
- 8 tablespoons (1 stick) butter, melted

1. Preheat the oven to 170 .
2. Put the nuts on a baking tray. Toast the nuts for 5 minutes.
3. Put the desiccated coconut on a clean baking tray; toast just until it turns golden brown, about 3 to 5 minutes (coconut burns fast so keep an eye on it). Once done, remove it from the oven and put it in a shallow bowl.
4. In a food processor fitted with a chopping blade, process the nuts until they have a medium chop.
5. Put the chopped nuts into a medium bowl.
6. Add the dates and melted butter to the food processor and blend until the dates become a thick paste.
7. Pour the chopped nuts into the food processor with the dates and pulse just until the mixture is combined, about 5 to 7 pulses.
8. Remove the mixture from the food processor and scrape it into a large bowl.
9. To make the balls, spoon 1 to 2 tablespoons of the date mixture into the palm of your hand and roll around between your hands until you form a ball.
10. Put the ball on a clean, lined baking tray. Repeat until all the mixture is formed into balls.
11. Roll each ball in the toasted coconut until the outside of the ball is coated, put the ball back on the baking tray, and repeat.
12. Put all the balls into the fridge for 20 minutes before serving so that they firm up.
13. You can also store any leftovers in the fridge in an airtight container.

Chocolate Turtle Hummus
Prep time: 5 minutes|Cook time:15 minutes|Serves 2

- For the caramel
- 2 tablespoons coconut oil
- 1 tablespoon maple syrup
- 1 tablespoon almond butter
- Pinch salt
- For the hummus
- ½ cup chickpeas, drained and rinsed
- 2 tablespoons unsweetened cocoa powder
- 1 tablespoon maple syrup, plus more to taste
- 2 tablespoons almond milk, or more as needed, to thin
- Pinch salt
- 2 tablespoons pecans

TO MAKE THE CARAMEL
1. To make the caramel, put the coconut oil in a small microwave-safe bowl. If it's solid, microwave it for about 15 seconds to melt it.
2. Stir in the maple syrup, almond butter, and salt.
3. Place the caramel in the refrigerator for 5 to 10 minutes to thicken.

TO MAKE THE HUMMUS
1. In a food processor, combine the chickpeas, cocoa powder, maple syrup, almond milk, and pinch of salt, and process until smooth. Scrape down the sides to make sure everything is incorporated.
2. If the hummus seems too thick, add another tablespoon of almond milk.
3. Add the pecans and pulse 6 times to roughly chop them.
4. Transfer the hummus to a serving bowl and when the caramel is thickened, swirl it into the hummus. Gently fold it in, but don't mix it in completely.
5. Serve with fresh fruit or pretzels.

Avocado-Orange Fruit Salad

Prep time: 10 minutes|Cook time:30 minutes|Serves 6

- 2 large Gala apples, chopped
- 2 oranges, segmented and chopped
- ⅓ cup rasherd almonds
- ½ cup honey
- 1 tablespoon extra-virgin olive oil
- ½ teaspoon grated orange zest
- 1 large avocado, semi-ripened, medium diced

1. In a large bowl, combine the apples, oranges, and almonds. Mix gently.
2. In a small bowl, whisk the honey, oil, and orange zest. Set aside.
3. Drizzle the orange zest mix over the fruit salad and toss.
4. Add the avocado and toss gently one more time.

Shortbread with Strawberry Preserves

Prep time: 20 minutes|Cook time:10 minutes|Serves 3

- 2 cups cornflour
- 1½ cups plain flour
- 2 teaspoons baking powder
- 1 teaspoon bicarbonate of soda
- 1 cup (2 sticks) cold butter, cut into 1-inch cubes
- ⅔ cup sugar
- 4 large egg yolks
- 2 tablespoons brandy
- 1 teaspoon vanilla extract
- ½ teaspoon salt
- 2 cups strawberry preserves
- Icing sugar, for sprinkling

1. In a bowl, combine the cornflour, flour, baking powder, and bicarbonate of soda and mix together.
2. Using your hands or 2 forks, mix the butter and sugar just until combined, with small pieces of butter remaining.
3. Add the egg yolks, brandy, vanilla, and salt, stirring slowly until all ingredients are blended together.
4. If you have a stand mixer, you can mix these ingredients together with the paddle attachment and then finish mixing by hand, but it is not required.
5. Wrap the dough in cling film and place in a resealable plastic bag for at least 1 hour.
6. Preheat the oven to 170 .
7. Roll the dough to ¼-inch thickness and cut, placing 12 Scones on a sheet.
8. Bake the sheets one at a time on the top rack of the oven for 12 to 14 minutes.
9. Let the Scones cool completely and top with about 1 tablespoon of strawberry preserves.
10. Sprinkle with icing sugar.

Orange Olive Oil Fairy cakes

Prep time: 15 minutes|Cook time:20 minutes|Serves 6

- 1 large egg
- 2 tablespoons icing sugar-free sweetener (such as stevia or monk fruit extract)
- ½ cup extra-virgin olive oil
- 1 teaspoon almond extract
- Zest of 1 orange
- 1 cup almond flour
- ¾ teaspoon baking powder
- ⅛ teaspoon salt
- 1 tablespoon freshly squeezed orange juice

1. Preheat the oven to 170 .
2. Place muffin liners into 6 cups of a muffin tin.
3. In a large bowl, whisk together the egg and powdered sweetener.
4. Add the olive oil, almond extract, and orange zest and whisk to combine well.
5. In a small bowl, whisk together the almond flour, baking powder, and salt.
6. Add to wet ingredients along with the orange juice and stir until just combined.
7. Divide the batter evenly into 6 muffin cups and bake until a toothpick inserted in the center of the Fairy cake comes out clean, 15 to 18 minutes.
8. Remove from the oven and cool for 5 minutes in the tin before transferring to a wire rack to cool completely.

Olive Oil Ice Cream

Prep time: 5 minutes, plus 12 to 24 hours|Cook time:25 minutes, plus 6 hourss|Serves 8

- 4 large egg yolks
- ⅓ cup icing sugar-free sweetener (such as stevia or monk fruit extract)
- 2 cups single cream or 1 cup heavy whipping cream and 1 cup whole milk
- 1 teaspoon vanilla extract
- ⅛ teaspoon salt
- ¼ cup light fruity extra-virgin olive oil

1. Freeze the bowl of an ice cream maker for at least 12 hours or overnight.
2. In a large bowl, whisk together the egg yolks and sugar-free sweetener.
3. Slowly pour the warm single cream into the egg mixture, whisking constantly to avoid cooking the eggs. Return the eggs and cream to the saucepan over low heat.
4. Whisking constantly, cook over low heat until thickened, 15 to 20 minutes.
5. Remove from the heat and stir in the vanilla essenceand salt.
6. Whisk in the olive oil and transfer to a glass bowl.
7. Allow to cool, cover, and refrigerate for at least 6 hours.
8. Freeze custard in an ice cream maker according to manufacturer's directions.

Stuffed Figs with Goat Cheese and Honey

Prep time: 5 minutes|Cook time:10 minutes|Serves 4

- 8 fresh figs
- 2 ounces goat cheese
- ¼ teaspoon ground cinnamon
- 1 tablespoon honey, plus more for serving
- 1 tablespoon olive oil

1. Preheat the air fryer to 180 .
2. Cut the stem off of each fig.
3. Cut an X into the top of each fig, cutting halfway down the fig. Leave the base intact.
4. In a small bowl, mix together the goat cheese, cinnamon, and honey.
5. Spoon the goat cheese mixture into the cavity of each fig.
6. Place the figs in a single layer in the air fryer basket.
7. Drizzle the olive oil over top of the figs and roast for 10 minutes.
8. Serve with an additional drizzle of honey.

Lemon Panna Cotta With Blackberries

Prep time: 20 minutes|Cook time:10 minutes, plus 6 hours|Serves 2

- ¾ cup single cream, divided
- 1 teaspoon unflavored powdered gelatin
- ½ cup heavy cream
- 3 tablespoons sugar
- 1 teaspoon lemon zest
- 1 tablespoon freshly squeezed lemon juice
- 1 teaspoon lemon extract
- ½ cup fresh blackberries
- Lemon peels to garnish (optional)

1. Place ¼ cup of single cream in a small bowl.
2. Sprinkle the gelatin powder evenly over the single cream and set it aside for 10 minutes to hydrate.
3. In a saucepan, combine the remaining ½ cup of single cream, the heavy cream, sugar, lemon zest, lemon juice, and lemon extract.
4. Heat the mixture over medium heat for 4 minutes, or until it's barely simmering—don't let it come to a full boil.
5. Remove from the heat.
6. When the gelatin is hydrated (it will look like applesauce), add it into the warm cream mixture, whisking as the gelatin melts.
7. If there are any remaining clumps of gelatin, sieve the liquid or remove the lumps with a spoon.
8. Pour the mixture into 2 dessert glasses or stemless wineglasses and refrigerate for at least 6 hours, or up to overnight.
9. Serve with the fresh berries and garnish with some strips of fresh lemon peel, if desired.

Roasted Pears with Dried Apricots and Pistachios

Prep time: 5 minutes|Cook time:10 minutes|Serves 4 to 6

- 2 tablespoons extra-virgin olive oil
- 4 ripe but firm Bosc or Bartlett pears (6 to 7 ounces each), peeled, halved, and cored
- 1¼ cups dry white wine
- ½ cup dried apricots, quartered
- ⅓ cup sugar
- ¼ teaspoon ground cardamom
- ⅛ teaspoon salt
- 1 teaspoon lemon juice
- ⅓ cup shelled pistachios, toasted and chopped

1. Adjust oven rack to middle position and heat oven to 225 .
2. Heat oil in 12-inch ovensafe frying pan over medium-high heat until shimmering.
3. Place pears cut side down in frying pan and cook, without moving them, until just beginning to brown, 3 to 5 minutes.
4. Transfer frying pan to oven and roast pears for 15 minutes.
5. Being careful of hot frying pan handle, flip pears and continue to roast until toothpick slips easily in and out of pears, 10 to 15 minutes.
6. Using potholders, remove frying pan from oven and carefully transfer pears to serving platter.
7. Add wine, apricots, sugar, cardamom, and salt to now-empty frying pan and bring to simmer over medium-high heat.
8. Cook, whisking to scrape up any browned bits, until sauce is reduced and has consistency of maple syrup, 7 to 10 minutes. Off heat, stir in lemon juice.
9. Pour sauce over pears and sprinkle with pistachios.
10. Serve.

Appendix 1 Measurement Conversion Chart

Volume Equivalents (Dry)	
US STANDARD	**METRIC (APPROXIMATE)**
1/8 teaspoon	0.5 mL
1/4 teaspoon	1 mL
1/2 teaspoon	2 mL
3/4 teaspoon	4 mL
1 teaspoon	5 mL
1 tablespoon	15 mL
1/4 cup	59 mL
1/2 cup	118 mL
3/4 cup	177 mL
1 cup	235 mL
2 cups	475 mL
3 cups	700 mL
4 cups	1 L

Volume Equivalents (Liquid)		
US STANDARD	**US STANDARD (OUNCES)**	**METRIC (APPROXIMATE)**
2 tablespoons	1 fl.oz.	30 mL
1/4 cup	2 fl.oz.	60 mL
1/2 cup	4 fl.oz.	120 mL
1 cup	8 fl.oz.	240 mL
1 1/2 cup	12 fl.oz.	355 mL
2 cups or 1 pint	16 fl.oz.	475 mL
4 cups or 1 quart	32 fl.oz.	1 L
1 gallon	128 fl.oz.	4 L

Temperatures Equivalents	
FAHRENHEIT(F)	**CELSIUS(C) APPROXIMATE)**
225 °F	107 °C
250 °F	120 ° °C
275 °F	135 °C
300 °F	150 °C
325 °F	160 °C
350 °F	180 °C
375 °F	190 °C
400 °F	205 °C
425 °F	220 °C
450 °F	235 °C
475 °F	245 °C
500 °F	260 °C

Weight Equivalents	
US STANDARD	**METRIC (APPROXIMATE)**
1 ounce	28 g
2 ounces	57 g
5 ounces	142 g
10 ounces	284 g
15 ounces	425 g
16 ounces (1 pound)	455 g
1.5 pounds	680 g
2 pounds	907 g

Appendix 2 The Dirty Dozen and Clean Fifteen

The Environmental Working Group (EWG) is a nonprofit, nonpartisan organization dedicated to protecting human health and the environment Its mission is to empower people to live healthier lives in a healthier environment. This organization publishes an annual list of the twelve kinds of produce, in sequence, that have the highest amount of pesticide residue-the Dirty Dozen-as well as a list of the fifteen kinds ofproduce that have the least amount of pesticide residue-the Clean Fifteen.

THE DIRTY DOZEN	
The 2016 Dirty Dozen includes the following produce. These are considered among the year's most important produce to buy organic:	
Strawberries	Spinach
Apples	Tomatoes
Nectarines	Bell peppers
Peaches	Cherry tomatoes
Celery	Cucumbers
Grapes	Kale/collard greens
Cherries	Hot peppers
The Dirty Dozen list contains two additional itemskale/collard greens and hot peppers-because they tend to contain trace levels of highly hazardous pesticides.	

THE CLEAN FIFTEEN	
The least critical to buy organically are the Clean Fifteen list. The following are on the 2016 list:	
Avocados	Papayas
Corn	Kiw
Pineapples	Eggplant
Cabbage	Honeydew
Sweet peas	Grapefruit
Onions	Cantaloupe
Asparagus	Cauliflower
Mangos	
Some of the sweet corn sold in the United States are made from genetically engineered (GE) seedstock. Buy organic varieties of these crops to avoid GE produce.	

Appendix 3 Index

A

all-purpose flour 50, 53
allspice 15
almond 5, 14
ancho chile 10
ancho chile powder 5
apple 9
apple cider vinegar 9
arugula 51
avocado 11

B

bacon 52
balsamic vinegar 7, 12, 52
basil 5, 8, 11, 13
beet 52
bell pepper 50, 51, 53
black beans 50, 51
broccoli 51, 52, 53
buns 52
butter 50

C

canola oil 50, 51, 52
carrot 52, 53
cauliflower 5, 52
cayenne 5, 52
cayenne pepper 52
Cheddar cheese 52
chicken 6
chili powder 50, 51
chipanle pepper 50
chives 5, 6, 52
cinnamon 15
coconut 6
Colby Jack cheese 51
coriander 52
corn 50, 51
corn kernels 50
cumin 5, 10, 15, 50, 51, 52

D

diced panatoes 50
Dijon mustard 7, 12, 13, 51
dry onion powder 52

E

egg 14, 50, 53
enchilada sauce 51

F

fennel seed 53
flour 50, 53
fresh chives 5, 6, 52
fresh cilantro 52
fresh cilantro leaves 52
fresh dill 5
fresh parsley 6, 52
fresh parsley leaves 52

G

garlic 5, 9, 10, 11, 13, 14, 50, 51, 52, 53
garlic powder 8, 9, 52, 53

H

half-and-half 50
hemp seeds 8
honey 9, 51

I

instant rice 51

K

kale 14
kale leaves 14
ketchup 53
kosher salt 5, 10, 15

L

lemon 5, 6, 14, 51, 53
lemon juice 6, 8, 11, 13, 14, 51
lime 9, 12
lime juice 9, 12
lime zest 9, 12

M

maple syrup 7, 12, 53
Marinara Sauce 5
micro greens 52
milk 5, 50
mixed berries 12
Mozzarella 50, 53
Mozzarella cheese 50, 53
mushroom 51, 52
mustard 51, 53
mustard powder 53

N

nutritional yeast 5

O

olive oil 5, 12, 13, 14, 50, 51, 52, 53
onion 5, 50, 51
onion powder 8
oregano 5, 8, 10, 50

P

panatoes 50, 52
paprika 5, 15, 52
Parmesan cheese 51, 53
parsley 6, 52
pesto 52
pink Himalayan salt 5, 7, 8, 11
pizza dough 50, 53
pizza sauce 50
plain coconut yogurt 6
plain Greek yogurt 5
porcini powder 53
potato 53

R

Ranch dressing 52
raw honey 9, 12, 13
red pepper flakes 5, 8, 14, 15, 51, 53
ricotta cheese 53

S

saffron 52
Serrano pepper 53
sugar 10
summer squash 51

T

tahini 5, 8, 9, 11
thyme 50
toasted almonds 14
tomato 5, 50, 52, 53
turmeric 15

U

unsalted butter 50
unsweetened almond milk 5

V

vegetable broth 50
vegetable stock 51

W

white wine 8, 11
wine vinegar 8, 10, 11

Y

yogurt 5, 6

Z

zucchini 50, 51, 52, 53

LAVERNE S. SPICER

Printed in Great Britain
by Amazon

20133646R00045